SMART AIR FRYER OVEN
COOKBOOK FOR BEGINNERS

Amazingly Easy Recipes to Fry, Bake, Grill, and Roast with Your Smart Air Fryer Oven

KATHERINE HOWARD

Copyright

No part of this publication may be reproduced, stored in a retrieval system or transmitted in any form or by any means, electronic, mechanical, photocopying, recording, scanning or otherwise, except as permitted under Sections 107 or 108 of the 1976 United States Copyright Act, without the prior written permission of the Publisher. Requests to the Publisher for permission should be addressed to the Permissions Department.

Limit of Liability/Disclaimer of Warranty: The Publisher and the author make no representations or warranties with respect to the accuracy or completeness of the contents of this work and specifically disclaim all warranties, including without limitation warranties of fitness for a particular purpose. No warranty may be created or extended by sales or promotional materials. The advice and strategies contained herein may not be suitable for every situation. This work is sold with the understanding that the publisher is not engaged in rendering medical, legal or other professional advice or services.

If professional assistance is required, the services of a competent professional person should be sought. Neither the Publisher nor the author shall be liable for damages arising here from. The fact that an individual, organization or website is referred to in this work as a citation and/or potential source of further information does not mean that the author or the Publisher endorses the information the individual, organization or website may provide or recommendations they/it may make. Further, readers should be aware that Internet websites listed in this work might have changed or disappeared between when this work was written and when it is read.
The author publishes its books in a variety of electronic and print formats. Some content that appears in print may not be available in electronic books, and vice versa.

TRADEMARKS: All other trademarks are the property of their respective owners. The author is not associated with any product or vendor mentioned in this book.

Table Of Contents

Table Of Contents ... 4

INTRODUCTION ... 8

Vegetables Recipes ... 10

   Parmesan Breaded Zucchini Chips ... 10

   Spicy Sweet Potato FriesPotato Fries ... 12

   Stuffed Mushrooms ... 13

   Air Fried Carrots, Yellow Squash & Zucchini ... 14

   Winter Vegetarian Frittata ... 15

   Air Fried Kale Chips ... 16

   Cheesy Cauliflower Fritters ... 17

   Cauliflower Bites ... 18

   Roasted Vegetables Salad ... 19

   Zucchini Parmesan Chips ... 21

   Jalapeño Cheese Balls ... 22

   Buffalo Cauliflower ... 23

   Onion Rings ... 24

Poultry Recipes ... 25

   Perfect Chicken Parmesan ... 25

   Honey and Wine Chicken Breasts ... 27

   Crispy Honey Garlic Chicken Wings ... 28

   Chicken-Fried Steak Supreme ... 29

   Cheesy Chicken Tenders ... 30

   Lemon-Pepper Chicken Wings ... 31

   Cheesy Chicken in Leek-Tomato Sauce ... 32

   Mexican Chicken Burgers ... 33

   Minty Chicken-Fried Pork Chops ... 34

   Fried Chicken Livers ... 35

   Crispy Southern Fried Chicken ... 36

   Tex-Mex Turkey Burgers ... 37

Air Fryer Turkey Breast	*38*
Mustard Chicken Tenders	*39*
Chicken Nuggets	*40*
Cheesy Chicken Fritters	*41*
Air Fryer Chicken Parmesan	*42*
Ricotta and Parsley Stuffed Turkey Breasts	*43*

Pork Recipes — 44

Barbecue Flavored Pork Ribs	*44*
Rustic Pork Ribs	*45*
Pork Wonton Wonderful	*46*
Italian Parmesan Breaded Pork Chops	*47*
Crispy Breaded Pork Chops	*48*
Caramelized Pork Shoulder	*49*
Roasted Pork Tenderloin	*50*
Pork Cutlet Rolls	*51*
Bacon Wrapped Pork Tenderloin	*52*
Dijon Garlic Pork Tenderloin	*53*
Pork Neck with Salad	*54*
Chinese Braised Pork Belly	*55*
Air Fryer Sweet and Sour Pork	*56*
Fried Pork Scotch Egg	*57*
Juicy Pork Ribs Ole	*59*
Teriyaki Pork Rolls	*60*

Beef Recipes — 61

Spicy Thai Beef Stir-Fry	*61*
Copycat Taco Bell Crunch Wraps	*62*
Meat Lovers' Pizza	*63*
Country Fried Steak	*64*
Beef & veggie Spring Rolls	*65*
Air Fryer Roast Beef	*66*
Crispy Mongolian Beef	*67*
Swedish Meatballs	*68*

Tender Beef with Sour Cream Sauce	69
Air Fryer Burgers	70
Carrot and Beef Cocktail Balls	71
Beef Steaks with Beans	72
Mushroom Meatloaf	73

Seafood Recipes — 74

Bacon Wrapped Shrimp	74
Crispy Paprika Fish Fillets	75
Air Fryer Salmon	76
Sweet And Savory Breaded Shrimp	77
Quick Paella	78
Coconut Shrimp	79
Cilantro-Lime Fried Shrimp	80
Lemony Tuna	81
Grilled Soy Salmon Fillets	82
Old Bay Crab Cakes	83
Scallops and Spring Veggies	84
Fried Calamari	85
Soy and Ginger Shrimp	86
Crispy Cheesy Fish Fingers	87
Panko-Crusted Tilapia	88
Fish Cakes With Mango Relish	89
Firecracker Shrimp	90
Sesame Seeds Coated Fish	91
Crispy Paprika Fish Fillets	92
Parmesan Shrimp	93
Fish and Chips	94
Crab Cakes	95

Sweet Recipes — 96

Fried Peaches	96
Apple Dumplings	97
Raspberry Cream Rol-Ups	98

Air Fryer Chocolate Cake — *99*

Chocolate Donuts — *100*

Fried Bananas with Chocolate Sauce — *101*

Apple Hand Pies — *102*

Chocolaty Banana Muffins — *103*

Blueberry Lemon Muffins — *104*

Sweet Cream Cheese Wontons — *105*

Air Fryer Cinnamon Rolls — *106*

Black and White Brownies — *107*

Baked Apple — *108*

Cinnamon Fried Bananas — *109*

HERITAGE OF FOOD: A FAMILY GATHERING — **110**

About the Author — **111**

INTRODUCTION

The Air fryer oven is an easy way to cook delicious healthy meals. Rather than cooking the food in oil and hot fat that may affect your health, the machine uses rapid hot air to circulate around and cook meals. This allows the outside of your food to be crispy and also makes sure that the inside layers are cooked through.

Air fryer oven allows us to cook almost everything and a lot of dishes. We can use the Air fryer oven to cook Meat, vegetables, poultry, fruit, fish and a wide variety of desserts. It is possible to prepare your entire meals, starting from appetizers to main courses as well as desserts. Not to mention, Air fryer oven also allows home prepared preserves or even delicious sweets and cakes.

How Does Air fryer oven Works?

The technology of the Air fryer oven is very simple. Fried foods get their crunchy texture because hot oil heats foods quickly and evenly on their surface. Oil is an excellent heat conductor, which helps with fast and simultaneous cooking across all of the ingredients. For decades cooks have used convection ovens to try to mimic the effects of frying or cooking the whole surface of food. But the air never circulates quickly enough to achieve that delicious surface crisp we all love in fried foods.
With this mechanism the air is circulated on high degrees, up to 200° C, to "air fry" any food such as fish, chicken or chips etc. This technology has changed the whole idea of cooking by reducing the fat up to 80% compared to old-fashioned deep fat frying.
The Air fryer oven cooking releases the heat through a heating element which cooks the food in a healthier and more appropriate way. There's also an exhaust fan right above the cooking chamber which provides the food required airflow. This way food is cooked with constant heated air. This leads to the same heating temperature reaching every single part of the food that is being cooked. So, this is only grill and the exhaust fan that is helping the Air fryer oven to boost air at a constantly high speed in order to cook healthy food with less fat.
The internal pressure increases the temperature that will then be controlled by the exhaust system. Exhaust fan also releases filtered extra air to cook the food in a much healthier way. Air fryer oven has no odor at all and it is absolutely harmless making it user and environment friendly.

Benefits of the Air fryer oven

- Healthier, oil-free meals
- It eliminates cooking odors through internal air filters
- Makes cleaning easier due to lack of oil grease
- Air Fryers are able to bake, grill, roast and fry providing more options
- Safer method of cooking compared to deep frying with exposed hot oil
- Has the ability to set and leave as most models and it includes a digital timer

The Air fryer oven is an all-in-one that allows cooking to be easy and quick. It also leads to a lot of possibilities once you get to know it. Once you learn the basics and become familiar with your Air fryer oven, you can feel free to experiment and modify the recipes in the way you prefer. You can prepare a wide number of dishes in the Air fryer oven and you can adapt your favorite stove-top dish so it becomes air fryer–friendly. It all boils down to variety and lots of options, right?

Cooking perfect and delicious as well as healthy meals has never been easier. You can see how this recipe collection proves itself.

Enjoy!

Vegetables Recipes

Parmesan Breaded Zucchini Chips
PREP: 15 MINUTES • COOK TIME: 20 MINUTES • TOTAL: 35 MINUTES
SERVES: 5

Ingredients
For the zucchini chips:
2 medium zucchini
2 eggs
⅓ cup bread crumbs
⅓ cup grated Parmesan cheese
Salt
Pepper
Cooking oil

For the lemon aioli:
½ cup mayonnaise
½ tablespoon olive oil
Juice of ½ lemon
1 teaspoon minced garlic
Salt
Pepper

Directions
1. **Preparing the Ingredients.** To make the zucchini chips:
   Slice the zucchini into thin chips (about ⅛ inch thick) using a knife or mandoline.
   In a small bowl, beat the eggs. In another small bowl, combine the bread crumbs, Parmesan cheese, and salt and pepper to taste.
   Spray the Oven rack/basket with cooking oil.
   Dip the zucchini slices one at a time in the eggs and then the bread crumb mixture. You can also sprinkle the bread crumbs onto the zucchini slices with a spoon.
   Place the zucchini chips in the Oven rack/basket, but do not stack. Place the Rack on the middle-shelf of the Air fryer oven.
2. **Air Frying.** Cook in batches. Spray the chips with cooking oil from a distance (otherwise, the breading may fly off). Cook for 10 minutes.
   Remove the cooked zucchini chips from the air fryer, then repeat step 5 with the remaining zucchini.

To make the lemon aioli:
While the zucchini is cooking, combine the mayonnaise, olive oil, lemon juice, and garlic in a small bowl, adding salt and pepper to taste. Mix well until fully combined.
Cool the zucchini and serve alongside the aioli.

PER SERVING: CALORIES: 192; FAT: 13G; PROTEIN: 6

Spicy Sweet Potato FriesPotato Fries
PREP: 5 MINUTES • COOK TIME: 37 MINUTES • TOTAL: 45 MINUTES
SERVES: 4

Ingredients
- 2 tbsp. sweet potato fry seasoning mix
- 2 tbsp. olive oil
- 2 sweet potatoes

Seasoning Mix:
- 2 tbsp. salt
- 1 tbsp. cayenne pepper
- 1 tbsp. dried oregano
- 1 tbsp. fennel
- 2 tbsp. coriander

Directions:
1. **Preparing the Ingredients.** Slice both ends off sweet potatoes and peel. Slice lengthwise in half and again crosswise to make four pieces from each potato.
Slice each potato piece into 2-3 slices, then slice into fries.
Grind together all of seasoning mix ingredients and mix in the salt.
Ensure the Air fryer oven is preheated to 350 degrees.
Toss potato pieces in olive oil, sprinkling with seasoning mix and tossing well to coat thoroughly.
2. **Air Frying.** Add fries to air fryer rack/basket. Set temperature to 350°F, and set time to 27 minutes. Select START/STOP to begin.
Take out the basket and turn fries. Turn off air fryer and let cook 10-12 minutes till fries are golden.

PER SERVING: CALORIES: 89; FAT: 14G; PROTEIN: 8Gs; SUGAR:3

Stuffed Mushrooms

PREP: 7 MINUTES • COOK TIME: 8 MINUTES • TOTAL: 15 MINUTES
SERVES: 12

Ingredients
2 Rashers Bacon, Diced
½ Onion, Diced
½ Bell Pepper, Diced
1 Small Carrot, Diced
24 Medium Size Mushrooms (Separate the caps & stalks)
1 cup Shredded Cheddar Plus Extra for the Top
½ cup Sour Cream

Directions:
1. **Preparing the Ingredients.** Chop the mushrooms stalks finely and fry them up with the bacon, onion, pepper and carrot at 350 ° for 8 minutes.

   When the veggies are fairly tender, stir in the sour cream & the cheese. Keep on the heat until the cheese has melted and everything is mixed nicely.

   Now grab the mushroom caps and heap a plop of filling on each one.

   Place in the fryer basket and top with a little extra cheese.

Air Fried Carrots, Yellow Squash & Zucchini

PREP: 5 MINUTES • COOK TIME: 35 MINUTES • TOTAL: 40 MINUTES
SERVES: 4

Ingredients
1 tbsp. chopped tarragon leaves
½ tsp. white pepper
1 tsp. salt
1 pound yellow squash
1 pound zucchini
6 tsp. olive oil
½ pound carrots

Directions:

1. **Preparing the Ingredients.** Stem and root the end of squash and zucchini and cut in ¾-inch half-moons. Peel and cut carrots into 1-inch cubes
Combine carrot cubes with 2 teaspoons of olive oil, tossing to combine.
2. **Air Frying.** Pour into the Oven rack/basket. Place the Rack on the middle-shelf of the Air fryer oven. Set temperature to 400°F, and set time to 5 minutes.
As carrots cook, drizzle remaining olive oil over squash and zucchini pieces, then season with pepper and salt. Toss well to coat.
Add squash and zucchini when the timer for carrots goes off. Cook 30 minutes, making sure to toss 2-3 times during the cooking process.
Once done, take out veggies and toss with tarragon. Serve up warm!

PER SERVING: CALORIES: 122; FAT: 9G; PROTEIN: 6G; SUGAR:0G

Winter Vegetarian Frittata

PREP: 5 MINUTES • COOK TIME: 30 MINUTES • TOTAL: 35 MINUTES
SERVES: 4

Ingredients

1 leek, peeled and thinly sliced into rings
2 cloves garlic, finely minced
3 medium-sized carrots, finely chopped
2 tablespoons olive oil
6 large-sized eggs
Sea salt and ground black pepper, to taste
1/2 teaspoon dried marjoram, finely minced
1/2 cup yellow cheese of choice

Directions:

1. **Preparing the Ingredients.** Sauté the leek, garlic, and carrot in hot olive oil until they are tender and fragrant; reserve.
   In the meantime, preheat your Air fryer oven to 330 degrees F.
   In a bowl, whisk the eggs along with the salt, ground black pepper, and marjoram.
   Then, grease the inside of your baking dish with a nonstick cooking spray. Pour the whisked eggs into the baking dish. Stir in the sautéed carrot mixture. Top with the cheese shreds.
2. **Air Frying.** Place the baking dish in the Air fryer oven cooking basket. Cook about 30 minutes and serve warm

Air Fried Kale Chips

PREP: 5 MINUTES • COOK TIME: 10 MINUTES • TOTAL: 15 MINUTES
SERVES: 6

Ingredients
¼ tsp. Himalayan salt
3 tbsp. yeast
Avocado oil
1 bunch of kale

Directions:

1. **Preparing the Ingredients.** Rinse kale and with paper towels, dry well.
   Tear kale leaves into large pieces. Remember they will shrink as they cook so good sized pieces are necessary.
   Place kale pieces in a bowl and spritz with avocado oil till shiny. Sprinkle with salt and yeast.
   With your hands, toss kale leaves well to combine.
2. **Air Frying.** Pour half of the kale mixture into the Air fryer oven, set temperature to 350°F, and set time to 5 minutes. Remove and repeat with another half of kale.

PER SERVING: CALORIES: 55; FAT: 10G; PROTEIN: 1G; SUGAR: 0G

Cheesy Cauliflower Fritters

PREP: 10 MINUTES • COOK TIME: 7 MINUTES • TOTAL: 17 MINUTES
SERVES: 8

Ingredients
½ C. chopped parsley
1 C. Italian breadcrumbs
1/3 C. shredded mozzarella cheese
1/3 C. shredded sharp cheddar cheese
1 egg
2 minced garlic cloves
3 chopped scallions
1 head of cauliflower

Directions:
1. **Preparing the Ingredients.** Cut the cauliflower up into florets. Wash well and pat dry. Place into a food processor and pulse 20-30 seconds till it looks like rice.
   Place cauliflower rice in a bowl and mix with pepper, salt, egg, cheeses, breadcrumbs, garlic, and scallions.
   With hands, form 15 patties of the mixture. Add more breadcrumbs if needed.
2. **Air Frying.** With olive oil, spritz patties, and place into your Air fryer oven in a single layer. Set temperature to 390°F, and set time to 7 minutes, flipping after 7 minutes.

PER SERVING: CALORIES: 209; FAT: 17G; PROTEIN: 6G; SUGAR:0.5

Cauliflower Bites

PREP: 10 MINUTES • COOK TIME: 18 MINUTES • TOTAL: 28 MINUTES
SERVES: 4

Ingredients
1 Head Cauliflower, cut into small florets
Tsps Garlic Powder
Pinch of Salt and Pepper
1 Tbsp Butter, melted
1/2 Cup Chili Sauce
Olive Oil

Directions:
1. **Preparing the Ingredients.** Place cauliflower into a bowl and pour oil over florets to lightly cover.
   Season florets with salt, pepper, and the garlic powder and toss well.
2. **Air Frying.** Place florets into the Air fryer oven at 350 degrees for 14 minutes.
   Remove cauliflower from the Air Fryer.
   Combine the melted butter with the chili sauce
   Pour over the florets so that they are well coated.
   Return to the Air fryer oven and cook for additional 3 to 4 minutes
   Serve as a side or with ranch or cheese dip as a snack.

Roasted Vegetables Salad

PREP: 5 MINUTES • COOK TIME: 85 MINUTES • TOTAL: 90 MINUTES
SERVES: 5

Ingredients

3 eggplants
1 tbsp of olive oil
3 medium zucchini
1 tbsp of olive oil
4 large tomatoes, cut them in eighths
4 cups of one shaped pasta
2 peppers of any color
1 cup of sliced tomatoes cut into small cubes
2 teaspoon of salt substitute
8 tbsp of grated parmesan cheese
½ cup of Italian dressing
Leaves of fresh basil

Directions:

1. **Preparing the Ingredients.** Wash your eggplant and slice it off then discard the green end. Make sure not to peel.
Slice your eggplant into 1/2 inch of thick rounds. 1/2 inch)
Pour 1tbsp of olive oil on the eggplant round.
2. **Air Frying.** Put the eggplants in the basket of the Air fryer oven and then toss it in the air fryer. Cook the eggplants for 40 minutes. Set the heat to 360 ° F
Meanwhile, wash your zucchini and slice it then discard the green end. But do not peel it. Slice the Zucchini into thick rounds of ½ inch each.
In the basket of the Air Fryer, toss your ingredients
Add 1 tbsp of olive oil.
3. **Air Frying.** Cook the zucchini for 25 minutes on a heat of 360° F and when the time is off set it aside.
Wash and cut the tomatoes.
4. **Air Frying.** Arrange your tomatoes in the basket of the Air fryer oven. Set the timer to 30 minutes. Set the heat to 350° F
When the time is off, cook your pasta according to the pasta guiding directions, empty it into a colander. Run the cold water on it and wash it and drain the pasta and put it aside.
Meanwhile, wash and chop your peppers and place it in a bow
Wash and thinly slice your cherry tomatoes and add it to the bowl. Add your roasted veggies.

Add the pasta, a pinch of salt, the topping dressing, add the basil and the parm and toss everything together. (It is better to mix with your hands). Set the ingredients together in the refrigerator, and let it chill
Serve your salad and enjoy it!

Zucchini Parmesan Chips

PREP: 10 MINUTES • COOK TIME: 8 MINUTES • TOTAL: 18 MINUTES
SERVES: 10

Ingredients
½ tsp. paprika
½ C. grated parmesan cheese
½ C. Italian breadcrumbs
1 lightly beaten egg
2 thinly sliced zucchinis

Directions:
1. **Preparing the Ingredients.** Use a very sharp knife or mandolin slicer to slice zucchini as thinly as you can. Pat off extra moisture.
   Beat egg with a pinch of pepper and salt and a bit of water.
   Combine paprika, cheese, and breadcrumbs in a bowl.
   Dip slices of zucchini into the egg mixture and then into breadcrumb mixture. Press gently to coat.
2. **Air Frying**. With olive oil cooking spray, mist coated zucchini slices. Place into your Air fryer oven in a single layer. Set temperature to 350°F, and set time to 8 minutes. Sprinkle with salt and serve with salsa.

PER SERVING: CALORIES: 211; FAT: 16G; PROTEIN:8G; SUGAR:0G

Jalapeño Cheese Balls

PREP: 10 MINUTES • **COOK TIME:** 8 MINUTES • **TOTAL:** 18 MINUTES
SERVES: 12

Ingredients
4 ounces cream cheese
⅓ cup shredded mozzarella cheese
⅓ cup shredded Cheddar cheese
2 jalapeños, finely chopped
½ cup bread crumbs
2 eggs
½ cup all-purpose flour
Salt
Pepper
Cooking oil

Directions:
1. **Preparing the Ingredients.** In a medium bowl, combine the cream cheese, mozzarella, Cheddar, and jalapeños. Mix well.
   Form the cheese mixture into balls about an inch thick. Using a small ice cream scoop works well.
   Arrange the cheese balls on a sheet pan and place in the freezer for 15 minutes. This will help the cheese balls maintain their shape while frying.
   Spray the Oven rack/basket with cooking oil. Place the bread crumbs in a small bowl. In another small bowl, beat the eggs. In a third small bowl, combine the flour with salt and pepper to taste, and mix well. Remove the cheese balls from the freezer. Dip the cheese balls in the flour, then the eggs, and then the bread crumbs.
2. **Air Frying**. Place the cheese balls in the Oven rack/basket. Spray with cooking oil. Place the Rack on the middle-shelf of the Air fryer oven. Cook for 8 minutes.
   Open the air fryer and flip the cheese balls. I recommend flipping them instead of shaking, so the balls maintain their form. Cook an additional 4 minutes. Cool before serving.

PER SERVING: CALORIES: 96; FAT: 6G; PROTEIN:4G; SUGAR:

Buffalo Cauliflower

PREP: 5 MINUTES • COOK TIME: 15 MINUTES • TOTAL: 20 MINUTES
SERVES: 2

Ingredients
Cauliflower:
1 C. panko breadcrumbs
1 tsp. salt
4 C. cauliflower florets
Buffalo Coating:
¼ C. Vegan Buffalo sauce
¼ C. melted vegan butter

Directions:
1. **Preparing the Ingredients.** Melt butter in microwave and whisk in buffalo sauce.
   Dip each cauliflower floret into buffalo mixture, ensuring it gets coated well. Hold over a bowl till floret is done dripping.
   Mix breadcrumbs with salt.
2. **Air Frying**. Dredge dipped florets into breadcrumbs and place into the air fryer. Set the temperature to 350°F, and set time to 15 minutes. When slightly browned, they are ready to eat!
   Serve with your favorite keto dipping sauce!

PER SERVING: CALORIES: 194; FAT: 17G; PROTEIN:10G; SUGAR:

Onion Rings

PREP: 10 MINUTES • COOK TIME: 10 MINUTES • TOTAL: 20 MINUTES
SERVES: 4

Ingredients
1 large spanish onion
1/2 cup buttermilk
2 eggs, lightly beaten
3/4 cups unbleached all-purpose flour
3/4 cups panko bread crumbs
1/2 teaspoon baking powder
1/2 teaspoon Cayenne pepper, to taste
Salt

Directions:
1. **Preparing the Ingredients.** Start by cutting your onion into 1/2 thick rings and separate. Smaller pieces can be discarded or saved for other recipes.
   Beat the eggs in a large bowl and mix in the buttermilk, then set it aside.
   In another bowl combine flour, pepper, bread crumbs, and baking powder.
   Use a large spoon to dip a whole ring in the buttermilk, then pull it through the flour mix on both sides to completely coat the ring.
2. **Air Frying.** Cook about 8 rings at a time in your Air fryer oven for 8-10 minutes at 360 degrees shaking half way through.

PER SERVING: CALORIES: 225; FAT: 3.8G; PROTEIN:19G; FIBER:2.4G

Poultry Recipes

Perfect Chicken Parmesan
PREP: 5 MINUTES • COOK TIME: 25 MINUTES • TOTAL: 30 MINUTES
SERVES: 2

Ingredients
2 large white meat chicken breasts, approximately 5-6 ounces
1 cup of breadcrumbs (Panko brand works well)
2 medium-sized eggs
Pinch of salt and pepper
1 tablespoon of dried oregano
1 cup of marinara sauce (store-bought or homemade will do equally well)
2 slices of provolone cheese
1 tablespoon of parmesan cheese

Directions:
1. **Preparing the Ingredients.** Cover the basket of the Air fryer oven with a lining of tin foil, leaving the edges uncovered to allow air to circulate through the basket.
   Preheat the air fryer to 350 degrees.
   In a mixing bowl, beat the eggs until fluffy and until the yolks and whites are fully combined, and set aside.
   In a separate mixing bowl, combine the breadcrumbs, oregano, salt and pepper, and set aside.
   One by one, dip the raw chicken breasts into the bowl with dry ingredients, coating both sides; then submerge into the bowl with wet ingredients, then dip again into the dry ingredients. This double coating will ensure an extra crisp-and-delicious air-fry!
   Lay the coated chicken breasts on the foil covering the Oven rack/basket, in a single flat layer. Place the Rack on the middle-shelf of the Air fryer oven.
2. **Air Frying.** Set the Air fryer oven timer for 10 minutes.
   After 10 minutes, the air fryer will turn off and the chicken should be mid-way cooked and the breaded coating starting to brown.
   Using tongs, turn each piece of chicken over to ensure a full all-over fry.
   Reset the air fryer to 320 degrees for another 10 minutes.
   While the chicken is cooking, pour half the marinara sauce into a 7-inch heat-safe pan.

After 15 minutes, when the air fryer shuts off, remove the fried chicken breasts using tongs and set in the marinara-covered pan. Drizzle the rest of the marinara sauce over the fried chicken, then place the slices of provolone cheese atop both of them and sprinkle the parmesan cheese over the entire pan.

Reset the air fryer to 350 degrees for 5 minutes.

After 5 minutes, when the air fryer shuts off, remove the dish from the air fryer using tongs or oven mitts. The chicken will be perfectly crisped and the cheese melted and lightly toasted. Serve while hot!

Honey and Wine Chicken Breasts

PREP: 5 MINUTES • COOK TIME: 15 MINUTES • TOTAL: 20 MINUTES
SERVES: 4

Ingredients
2 chicken breasts, rinsed and halved
1 tablespoon melted butter
1/2 teaspoon freshly ground pepper, or to taste
3/4 teaspoon sea salt, or to taste
1 teaspoon paprika
1 teaspoon dried rosemary
2 tablespoons dry white wine
1 tablespoon honey

Directions:
1. **Preparing the Ingredients.** Firstly, pat the chicken breasts dry. Lightly coat them with the melted butter.
   Then, add the remaining ingredients.
2. **Air Frying.** Transfer them to the air fryer rack/basket; bake about 15 minutes at 330 degrees F. Serve warm and enjoy

PER SERVING: *CALORIES: 189; FAT: 14G; PROTEIN:11G; SUGAR:1*

Crispy Honey Garlic Chicken Wings

PREP: 10 MINUTES • COOK TIME: 25 MINUTES • TOTAL: 35 MINUTES
SERVES: 8

Ingredients
1/8 C. water
½ tsp. salt
4 tbsp. minced garlic
¼ C. vegan butter
¼ C. raw honey
¾ C. almond flour
16 chicken wings

Directions:
1. **Preparing the Ingredients.** Rinse off and dry chicken wings well.
Spray air fryer rack/basket with olive oil.
Coat chicken wings with almond flour and add coated wings to the Air fryer oven.
2. **Air Frying.** Set temperature to 380°F, and set time to 25 minutes. Cook shaking every 5 minutes.
When the timer goes off, cook 5-10 minutes at 400 degrees till skin becomes crispy and dry.
As chicken cooks, melt butter in a saucepan and add garlic. Sauté garlic 5 minutes. Add salt and honey, simmering 20 minutes. Make sure to stir every so often, so the sauce does not burn. Add a bit of water after 15 minutes to ensure sauce does not harden.
Take out chicken wings from air fryer and coat in sauce. Enjoy!

PER SERVING: CALORIES: 435; FAT: 19G; PROTEIN:31G; SUGAR:6

Chicken-Fried Steak Supreme

PREP: 10 MINUTES • COOK TIME: 30 MINUTES • TOTAL: 40 MINUTES
SERVES: 8

Ingredients
½ pound beef-bottom round, sliced into strips
1 cup of breadcrumbs (Panko brand works well)
2 medium-sized eggs
Pinch of salt and pepper
½ tablespoon of ground thyme

Directions:

1. **Preparing the Ingredients.** Cover the basket of the Air fryer oven with a lining of tin foil, leaving the edges uncovered to allow air to circulate through the basket. Preheat the air fryer to 350 degrees. In a mixing bowl, beat the eggs until fluffy and until the yolks and whites are fully combined, and set aside. In a separate mixing bowl, combine the breadcrumbs, thyme, salt and pepper, and set aside. One by one, dip each piece of raw steak into the bowl with dry ingredients, coating all sides; then submerge into the bowl with wet ingredients, then dip again into the dry ingredients. This double coating will ensure an extra crisp air fry. Lay the coated steak pieces on the foil covering the air-fryer basket, in a single flat layer.
2. **Air Frying.** Set the Air fryer oven timer for 15 minutes. After 15 minutes, the air fryer will turn off and the steak should be mid-way cooked and the breaded coating starting to brown. Using tongs, turn each piece of steak over to ensure a full all-over fry. Reset the air fryer to 320 degrees for 15 minutes. After 15 minutes, when the air fryer shuts off, remove the fried steak strips using tongs and set on a serving plate. Eat as soon as cool enough to handle and enjoy!

Cheesy Chicken Tenders

PREP: 10 MINUTES • COOK TIME: 30 MINUTES • TOTAL: 40 MINUTES
SERVES: 4

Ingredients

1 large white meat chicken breast, approximately 5-6 ounces, sliced into strips
1 cup of breadcrumbs (Panko brand works well)
2 medium-sized eggs
Pinch of salt and pepper
1 tablespoon of grated or powdered parmesan cheese

Directions:

1. **Preparing the Ingredients.** Cover the basket of the Air fryer oven with a lining of tin foil, leaving the edges uncovered to allow air to circulate through the basket. Preheat the Air fryer oven to 350 degrees. In a mixing bowl, beat the eggs until fluffy and until the yolks and whites are fully combined, and set aside. In a separate mixing bowl, combine the breadcrumbs, parmesan, salt, and pepper, and set aside. One by one, dip each piece of raw chicken into the bowl with dry ingredients, coating all sides; then submerge into the bowl with wet ingredients, then dip again into the dry ingredients. Lay the coated chicken pieces on the foil covering the Oven rack/basket, in a single flat layer. Place the Rack on the middle-shelf of the Air fryer oven.
2. **Air Frying.** Set the Air fryer oven timer for 15 minutes. After 15 minutes, the air fryer will turn off and the chicken should be mid-way cooked and the breaded coating starting to brown. Using tongs turn each piece of chicken over to ensure a full all over fry. Reset the air fryer to 320 degrees for another 15 minutes. After 15 minutes, when the air fryer shuts off, remove the fried chicken strips using tongs and set on a serving plate. Eat as soon as cool enough to handle, and enjoy!

PER SERVING: CALORIES: 278; FAT: 15G; PROTEIN:29G; SUGAR:7G

Lemon-Pepper Chicken Wings

PREP: 10 MINUTES • COOK TIME: 20 MINUTES • TOTAL: 30 MINUTES
SERVES: 4

Ingredients
8 whole chicken wings
Juice of ½ lemon
½ teaspoon garlic powder
1 teaspoon onion powder
Salt
Pepper
¼ cup low-fat buttermilk
½ cup all-purpose flour
Cooking oil

Directions:
1. **Preparing the Ingredients.** Place the wings in a sealable plastic bag. Drizzle the wings with the lemon juice. Season the wings with the garlic powder, onion powder, and salt and pepper to taste.
   Seal the bag. Shake thoroughly to combine the seasonings and coat the wings.
   Pour the buttermilk and the flour into separate bowls large enough to dip the wings.
   Spray the Oven rack/basket with cooking oil.
   One at a time, dip the wings in the buttermilk and then the flour.
2. **Air Frying.** Place the wings in the Oven rack/basket. It is okay to stack them on top of each other. Spray the wings with cooking oil, being sure to spray the bottom layer. Place the Rack on the middle-shelf of the Air fryer oven. Cook for 5 minutes.
   Remove the basket and shake it to ensure all of the pieces will cook fully.
   Return the basket to the Air fryer oven and continue to cook the chicken. Repeat shaking every 5 minutes until a total of 20 minutes has passed.
   Cool before serving.

PER SERVING: CALORIES: 347; FAT: 12G; PROTEIN:46G; FIBER:1G

Cheesy Chicken in Leek-Tomato Sauce

PREP: 10 MINUTES • COOK TIME: 20 MINUTES • TOTAL: 30 MINUTES
SERVES: 4

Ingredients
2 large-sized chicken breasts, cut in half lengthwise
Salt and ground black pepper, to taste
4 ounces Cheddar cheese, cut into sticks
1 tablespoon sesame oil
1 cup leeks, chopped
 2 cloves garlic, minced
2/3 cup roasted vegetable stock
2/3 cup tomato puree
1 teaspoon dried rosemary
1 teaspoon dried thyme

Directions:
1. **Preparing the Ingredients.** Firstly, season chicken breasts with the salt and black pepper; place a piece of Cheddar cheese in the middle. Then, tie it using a kitchen string; drizzle with sesame oil and reserve.
Add the leeks and garlic to the oven safe bowl.
2. **Air Frying.** Cook in the Air fryer oven at 390 degrees F for 5 minutes or until tender. Add the reserved chicken. Throw in the other ingredients and cook for 12 to 13 minutes more or until the chicken is done. Enjoy!

Mexican Chicken Burgers

PREP: 10 MINUTES • COOK TIME: 10 MINUTES • TOTAL: 20 MINUTES
SERVES: 6

Ingredients
1 jalapeno pepper
1 tsp. cayenne pepper
1 tbsp. mustard powder
1 tbsp. oregano
1 tbsp. thyme
3 tbsp. smoked paprika
1 beaten egg
1 small head of cauliflower
4 chicken breasts

Directions:
1. **Preparing the Ingredients.** Ensure your Air fryer oven is preheated to 350 degrees.
   Add seasonings to a blender. Slice cauliflower into florets and add to blender. Pulse till mixture resembles that of breadcrumbs.
   Take out ¾ of cauliflower mixture and add to a bowl. Set to the side. In another bowl, beat your egg and set to the side.
   Remove skin and bones from chicken breasts and add to blender with remaining cauliflower mixture. Season with pepper and salt.
   Take out mixture and form into burger shapes. Roll each patty in cauliflower crumbs, then the egg, and back into crumbs again.
2. **Air Frying.** Place coated patties into the Air fryer oven. Set temperature to 350°F, and set time to 10 minutes.
   Flip over at 10-minute mark. They are done when crispy!

PER SERVING: CALORIES: 234; FAT: 18G; PROTEIN:24G; SUGAR:1G

Minty Chicken-Fried Pork Chops

PREP: 10 MINUTES • COOK TIME: 30 MINUTES • TOTAL: 40 MINUTES
SERVES: 6

Ingredients

4 medium-sized pork chops, approximately 3.5 ounces each
1 cup of breadcrumbs (Panko brand works well)
2 medium-sized eggs
Pinch of salt and pepper
½ tablespoon of mint, either dried and ground; or fresh, rinsed and finely chopped

Directions:

1. **Preparing the Ingredients.** Cover the basket of the Air fryer oven with a lining of tin foil, leaving the edges uncovered to allow air to circulate through the basket. Preheat the Air fryer oven to 350 degrees.
   In a mixing bowl, beat the eggs until fluffy and until the yolks and whites are fully combined, and set aside.
   In a separate mixing bowl, combine the breadcrumbs, mint, salt, and pepper, and set aside. One by one, dip each raw pork chop into the bowl with dry ingredients, coating all sides; then submerge into the bowl with wet ingredients, then dip again into the dry ingredients. This double coating will ensure an extra crisp air-fry. Lay the coated pork chops on the foil covering the Oven rack/basket, in a single flat layer. Place the Rack on the middle-shelf of the Air fryer oven.
2. **Air Frying.** Set the Air fryer oven timer for 15 minutes. After 15 minutes, the Air fryer oven will turn off, and the pork should be mid-way cooked and the breaded coating starting to brown. Using tongs, turn each piece of steak over to ensure a full all-over fry. Reset the air fryer to 320 degrees for 15 minutes.
   After 15 minutes, when the air fryer shuts off, remove the fried pork chops using tongs and set on a serving plate. Eat as soon as cool enough to handle – and enjoy!

Fried Chicken Livers

PREP: 5 MINUTES • COOK TIME: 10 MINUTES • TOTAL: 15 MINUTES
SERVES: 4

Ingredients
1 pound chicken livers
1 cup flour
1/2 cup cornmeal
2 teaspoons your favorite seasoning blend
3 eggs
2 tablespoons milk

Directions:
1. **Preparing the Ingredients.** Clean and rinse the livers, pat dry.
   Beat eggs in a shallow bowl and mix in milk.
   In another bowl combine flour, cornmeal, and seasoning, mixing until even.
   Dip the livers in the egg mix, then toss them in the flour mix.
2. **Air Frying.** Air-fry at 375 degrees for 10 minutes using your Air fryer oven. Toss at least once halfway through.

PER SERVING: CALORIES: 409; FAT: 11G; PROTEIN:36G; FIBER:2G

Crispy Southern Fried Chicken

PREP: 10 MINUTES • COOK TIME: 25 MINUTES • TOTAL: 35 MINUTES
SERVES: 4

Ingredients
1 tsp. cayenne pepper
2 tbsp. mustard powder
2 tbsp. oregano
2 tbsp. thyme
3 tbsp. coconut milk
1 beaten egg
¼ C. cauliflower
¼ C. gluten-free oats
8 chicken drumsticks

Directions:
1. **Preparing the Ingredients.** Ensure the Air fryer oven is preheated to 350 degrees.
   Lay out chicken and season with pepper and salt on all sides.
   Add all other ingredients to a blender, blending till a smooth-like breadcrumb mixture is created. Place in a bowl and add a beaten egg to another bowl.
   Dip chicken into breadcrumbs, then into the egg, and breadcrumbs once more.
2. **Air Frying.** Place coated drumsticks into the Air fryer oven. Set temperature to 350°F, and set time to 20 minutes and cook 20 minutes. Bump up the temperature to 390 degrees and cook another 5 minutes till crispy.

PER SERVING: CALORIES: 504; FAT: 18G; PROTEIN:35G; SUGAR:5G

Tex-Mex Turkey Burgers

PREP: 10 MINUTES • COOK TIME: 15 MINUTES • TOTAL: 25 MINUTES
SERVES: 4

Ingredients
⅓ cup finely crushed corn tortilla chips
1 egg, beaten
¼ cup salsa
⅓ cup shredded pepper Jack cheese
Pinch salt
Freshly ground black pepper
1 pound ground turkey
1 tablespoon olive oil
1 teaspoon paprika

Directions:
1. **Preparing the Ingredients.** In a medium bowl, combine the tortilla chips, egg, salsa, cheese, salt, and pepper, and mix well.
   Add the turkey and mix gently but thoroughly with clean hands.
   Form the meat mixture into patties about ½ inch thick. Make an indentation in the center of each patty with your thumb, so the burgers don't puff up while cooking.
   Brush the patties on both sides with the olive oil and sprinkle with paprika.
2. **Air Frying.** Put in the Oven rack/basket. Place the Rack on the middle-shelf of the Air fryer oven. Grill for 14 to 16 minutes or until the meat registers at least 165°F.

PER SERVING: CALORIES: 354; FAT: 21G; PROTEIN:36G; FIBER:2G

Air Fryer Turkey Breast

PREP: 5 MINUTES • COOK TIME: 60 MINUTES • TOTAL: 65 MINUTES
SERVES: 6

Ingredients
Pepper and salt
1 oven-ready turkey breast
Turkey seasonings of choice

Directions:
1. **Preparing the Ingredients.** Preheat the Air fryer oven to 350 degrees. Season turkey with pepper, salt, and other desired seasonings. Place turkey in the Oven rack/basket. Place the Rack on the middle-shelf of the Air fryer oven.
2. **Air Frying.** Set temperature to 350°F, and set time to 60 minutes. Cook 60 minutes. The meat should be at 165 degrees when done. Allow to rest 10-15 minutes before slicing. Enjoy!

PER SERVING: CALORIES: 212; FAT: 12G; PROTEIN:24G; SUGAR:0G

Mustard Chicken Tenders

PREP: 5 MINUTES • COOK TIME: 20 MINUTES • TOTAL: 25 MINUTES
SERVES: 4

Ingredients
½ C. coconut flour
1 tbsp. spicy brown mustard
2 beaten eggs
1 pound of chicken tenders

Directions:
1. **Preparing the Ingredients.** Season tenders with pepper and salt. Place a thin layer of mustard onto tenders and then dredge in flour and dip in egg.
2. **Air Frying.** Add to the Air fryer oven, set temperature to 390°F, and set time to 20 minutes.

PER SERVING: CALORIES: 403; FAT: 20G; PROTEIN:22G; SUGAR:4G

Chicken Nuggets

PREP: 10 MINUTES • COOK TIME: 20 MINUTES • TOTAL: 30 MINUTES
SERVES: 4

Ingredients
1 pound boneless, skinless chicken breasts
Chicken seasoning or rub
Salt
Pepper
2 eggs
6 tablespoons bread crumbs
2 tablespoons panko bread crumbs
Cooking oil

Directions:
1. **Preparing the Ingredients.** Cut the chicken breasts into 1-inch pieces.
   In a large bowl, combine the chicken pieces with chicken seasoning, salt, and pepper to taste.
   In a small bowl, beat the eggs. In another bowl, combine the bread crumbs and panko.
   Dip the chicken pieces in the eggs and then the bread crumbs.
   Place the nuggets in the Air fryer oven. Do not overcrowd the basket. Cook in batches. Spray the nuggets with cooking oil.
2. **Air Frying.** Cook for 4 minutes. Open the Air fryer oven and shake the basket. Cook for an additional 4 minutes. Remove the cooked nuggets from the Air fryer oven, then repeat steps 5 and 6 for the remaining chicken nuggets. Cool before serving.

PER SERVING: CALORIES: 206; FAT: 5G; PROTEIN:31G; FIBER:1G

Cheesy Chicken Fritters
PREP: 5 MINUTES • COOK TIME: 20 MINUTES • TOTAL: 25 MINUTES
SERVES: 17 FRITTERS

Ingredients
Chicken Fritters:
½ tsp. salt
1/8 tsp. pepper
1 ½ tbsp. fresh dill
1 1/3 C. shredded mozzarella cheese
1/3 C. coconut flour
1/3 C. vegan mayo
2 eggs
1 ½ pounds chicken breasts
Garlic Dip:
1/8 tsp. pepper
¼ tsp. salt
½ tbsp. lemon juice
1 pressed garlic cloves
1/3 C. vegan mayo

Directions:

1. **Preparing the Ingredients.** Slice chicken breasts into 1/3" pieces and place in a bowl. Add all remaining fritter ingredients to the bowl and stir well. Cover and chill 2 hours or overnight.
   Ensure your air fryer is preheated to 350 degrees. Spray basket with a bit of olive oil.
2. **Air Frying.** Add marinated chicken to theAir fryer oven. Set temperature to 350°F, and set time to 20 minutes and cook 20 minutes, making sure to turn halfway through cooking process.
   To make the dipping sauce, combine all the dip ingredients until smooth.

PER SERVING: CALORIES: 467; FAT: 27G; PROTEIN:21G; SUGAR:3G

Air Fryer Chicken Parmesan

PREP: 5 MINUTES • COOK TIME: 9 MINUTES • TOTAL: 20 MINUTES
SERVES: 4

Ingredients
- ½ C. keto marinara
- 6 tbsp. mozzarella cheese
- 1 tbsp. melted ghee
- 2 tbsp. grated parmesan cheese
- 6 tbsp. gluten-free seasoned breadcrumbs
- 1 8-ounce chicken breasts

Directions:
1. **Preparing the Ingredients.** Ensure air fryer is preheated to 360 degrees. Spray the basket with olive oil.
   Mix parmesan cheese and breadcrumbs together. Melt ghee.
   Brush melted ghee onto the chicken and dip into breadcrumb mixture.
   Place coated chicken in the air fryer and top with olive oil.
2. **Air Frying.** Set temperature to 360°F, and set time to 6 minutes. Cook 2 breasts for 6 minutes and top each breast with a tablespoon of sauce and 1½ tablespoons of mozzarella cheese. Cook another 3 minutes to melt cheese.
   Keep cooked pieces warm as you repeat the process with remaining breasts.

PER SERVING: CALORIES: 251; FAT: 10G; PROTEIN:31G; SUGAR:0G

Ricotta and Parsley Stuffed Turkey Breasts

PREP: 5 MINUTES • COOK TIME: 25 MINUTES • TOTAL: 30 MINUTES
SERVES: 4

Ingredients

1 turkey breast, quartered
1 cup Ricotta cheese
1/4 cup fresh Italian parsley, chopped
1 teaspoon garlic powder
1/2 teaspoon cumin powder
1 egg, beaten
1 teaspoon paprika
Salt and ground black pepper, to taste
Crushed tortilla chips
1 ½ tablespoons extra-virgin olive oil

Directions:

1. **Preparing the Ingredients.** Firstly, flatten out each piece of turkey breast with a rolling pin. Prepare three mixing bowls.
   In a shallow bowl, combine Ricotta cheese with the parsley, garlic powder, and cumin powder.
   Place the Ricotta/parsley mixture in the middle of each piece. Repeat with the remaining pieces of the turkey breast and roll them up.
   In another shallow bowl, whisk the egg together with paprika. In the third shallow bowl, combine the salt, pepper, and crushed tortilla chips.
   Dip each roll in the whisked egg, then, roll them over the tortilla chips mixture.
   Transfer prepared rolls to the Oven rack/basket. Drizzle olive oil over all. Place the Rack on the middle-shelf of the Air fryer oven.
2. **Air Frying.** Cook at 350 degrees F for 25 minutes, working in batches. Serve warm, garnished with some extra parsley, if desired.

Pork Recipes

Barbecue Flavored Pork Ribs
PREP: 5 MINUTES • COOK TIME: 15 MINUTES • TOTAL: 25 MINUTES
SERVES: 6

Ingredients
¼ cup honey, divided
¾ cup BBQ sauce
2 tablespoons tomato ketchup
1 tablespoon Worcestershire sauce
1 tablespoon soy sauce
½ teaspoon garlic powder
Freshly ground white pepper, to taste
1¾ pound pork ribs

Directions:
1. **Preparing the Ingredients.** In a large bowl, mix together 3 tablespoons of honey and remaining ingredients except pork ribs.
   Refrigerate to marinate for about 20 minutes.
   Preheat the Air fryer oven to 355 degrees F.
   Place the ribs in an Air fryer rack/basket.
2. **Air Frying.** Cook for about 13 minutes.
   Remove the ribs from the Air fryer oven and coat with remaining honey.
   Serve hot.

Rustic Pork Ribs

PREP: 5 MINUTES • COOK TIME: 15 MINUTES • TOTAL: 25 MINUTES
SERVES: 4

Ingredients
1 rack of pork ribs
3 tablespoons dry red wine
1 tablespoon soy sauce
1/2 teaspoon dried thyme
1/2 teaspoon onion powder
1/2 teaspoon garlic powder
1/2 teaspoon ground black pepper
1 teaspoon smoke salt
1 tablespoon cornstarch
1/2 teaspoon olive oil

Directions:
1. **Preparing the Ingredients.** Begin by preheating your Air fryer oven to 390 degrees F. Place all ingredients in a mixing bowl and let them marinate at least 1 hour.
2. **Air Frying.** Cook the marinated ribs approximately 25 minutes at 390 degrees F. Serve hot.

Pork Wonton Wonderful

PREP: 10 MINUTES • COOK TIME: 25 MINUTES • TOTAL: 35 MINUTES
SERVES: 3

Ingredients

8 wanton wrappers (Leasa brand works great, though any will do)
4 ounces of raw minced pork
1 medium-sized green apple
1 cup of water, for wetting the wanton wrappers
1 tablespoon of vegetable oil
½ tablespoon of oyster sauce
1 tablespoon of soy sauce
Large pinch of ground white pepper

Directions:

1. **Preparing the Ingredients.** Cover the basket of the Air fryer oven with a lining of tin foil, leaving the edges uncovered to allow air to circulate through the basket. Preheat the air fryer to 350 degrees.
   In a small mixing bowl, combine the oyster sauce, soy sauce, and white pepper, then add in the minced pork and stir thoroughly. Cover and set in the fridge to marinate for at least 15 minutes. Core the apple, and slice into small cubes – smaller than bite-sized chunks.
   Add the apples to the marinating meat mixture, and combine thoroughly. Spread the wonton wrappers, and fill each with a large spoonful of the filling. Wrap the wontons into triangles, so that the wrappers fully cover the filling, and seal with a drop of the water.
   Coat each filled and wrapped wonton thoroughly with the vegetable oil, to help ensure a nice crispy fry. Place the wontons on the foil-lined air-fryer rack/basket. Place the Rack on the middle-shelf of the Air fryer oven.
2. **Air Frying.** Set the Air fryer oven timer to 25 minutes. Halfway through cooking time, shake the handle of the air fryer rack/basket vigorously to jostle the wontons and ensure even frying. After 25 minutes, when the Air fryer oven shuts off, the wontons will be crispy golden-brown on the outside and juicy and delicious on the inside. Serve directly from the Oven rack/basket and enjoy while hot.

Italian Parmesan Breaded Pork Chops

PREP: 5 MINUTES • COOK TIME: 25 MINUTES • TOTAL: 30 MINUTES
SERVES: 5

Ingredients

5 (3½- to 5-ounce) pork chops (bone-in or boneless)
1 teaspoon Italian seasoning
Seasoning salt
Pepper
¼ cup all-purpose flour
2 tablespoons Italian bread crumbs
3 tablespoons finely grated Parmesan cheese
Cooking oil

Directions:

1. **Preparing the Ingredients.** Season the pork chops with the Italian seasoning and seasoning salt and pepper to taste.
   Sprinkle the flour on both sides of the pork chops, then coat both sides with the bread crumbs and Parmesan cheese.
2. **Air Frying.** Place the pork chops in the Air fryer oven. Stacking them is okay. Spray the pork chops with cooking oil. Cook for 6 minutes.
   Open the Air fryer oven and flip the pork chops. Cook for an additional 6 minutes.
   Cool before serving. Instead of seasoning salt, you can use either chicken or pork rub for additional flavor. You can find these rubs in the spice aisle of the grocery store.

PER SERVING: CALORIES: 334; FAT: 7G; PROTEIN:34G; FIBER:0G

Crispy Breaded Pork Chops

PREP: 10 MINUTES • COOK TIME: 15 MINUTES • TOTAL: 25 MINUTES
SERVES: 8

Ingredients
1/8 tsp. pepper
¼ tsp. chili powder
½ tsp. onion powder
½ tsp. garlic powder
1 ¼ tsp. sweet paprika
2 tbsp. grated parmesan cheese
1/3 C. crushed cornflake crumbs
½ C. panko breadcrumbs
1 beaten egg
6 center-cut boneless pork chops

Directions:

1. **Preparing the Ingredients.** Ensure that your air fryer is preheated to 400 degrees. Spray the basket with olive oil.
   With ½ teaspoon salt and pepper, season both sides of pork chops.
   Combine ¾ teaspoon salt with pepper, chili powder, onion powder, garlic powder, paprika, cornflake crumbs, panko breadcrumbs, and parmesan cheese.
   Beat egg in another bowl.
   Dip pork chops into the egg and then crumb mixture.
   Add pork chops to air fryer and spritz with olive oil.
2. **Air Frying.** Set temperature to 400°F, and set time to 12 minutes. Cook 12 minutes, making sure to flip over halfway through the cooking process.
   Only add 3 chops in at a time and repeat the process with remaining pork chops.

PER SERVING: CALORIES: 378; FAT: 13G; PROTEIN:33G; SUGAR:1

Caramelized Pork Shoulder

PREP: 10 MINUTES • COOK TIME: 20 MINUTES • TOTAL: 30 MINUTES
SERVES: 8

Ingredients
1/3 cup soy sauce
2 tablespoons sugar
1 tablespoon honey
2 pound pork shoulder, cut into 1½-inch thick slices

Directions:

1. **Preparing the Ingredients**. In a bowl, mix together all ingredients except pork.
   Add pork and coat with marinade generously.
   Cover and refrigerate o marinate for about 2-8 hours.
   Preheat the Air fryer oven to 335 degrees F.
2. **Air Frying.** Place the pork in an Air fryer rack/basket.
   Cook for about 10 minutes.
   Now, set the Air fryer oven to 390 degrees F. Cook for about 10 minutes.

Roasted Pork Tenderloin

PREP: 5 MINUTES • COOK TIME: 1 HOUR • TOTAL: 65 MINUTES
SERVES: 4

Ingredients
1 (3-pound) pork tenderloin
2 tablespoons extra-virgin olive oil
2 garlic cloves, minced
1 teaspoon dried basil
1 teaspoon dried oregano
1 teaspoon dried thyme
Salt
Pepper

Directions:
1. **Preparing the Ingredients.** Drizzle the pork tenderloin with the olive oil. Rub the garlic, basil, oregano, thyme, and salt and pepper to taste all over the tenderloin.
2. **Air Frying**. Place the tenderloin in the Air fryer oven. Cook for 45 minutes.
Use a meat thermometer to test for doneness
Open the Air fryer oven and flip the pork tenderloin. Cook for an additional 15 minutes. Remove the cooked pork from the air fryer and allow it to rest for 10 minutes before cutting.

PER SERVING: CALORIES: 283; FAT: 10G; PROTEIN:48

Pork Cutlet Rolls

PREP: 10 MINUTES • COOK TIME: 15 MINUTES • TOTAL: 25 MINUTES
SERVES: 4

Ingredients
4 Pork Cutlets
4 Sundried Tomatoes in oil
2 Tbsps Parsley, finely chopped
1 Green Onion, finely chopped
Black Pepper to taste
2 Tsps Paprika
1/2 Tbsp Olive Oil
* String for Rolled Meat

Directions:
1. **Preparing the Ingredients.** Preheat the Air fryer oven to 390 degrees
   Finely chop the tomatoes and mix with the parsley and green onion. Add salt and pepper to taste
   Spread out the cutlets and coat them with the tomato mixture. Roll up the cutlets and secure intact with the string
   Rub the rolls with salt, pepper, and paprika powder and thinly coat them with olive oil
2. **Air Frying.** Put the cutlet rolls in the Air fryer oven tray and cook for 15 minutes. Roast until nicely brown and done.
   Serve with tomato sauce.

Bacon Wrapped Pork Tenderloin

PREP: 5 MINUTES • COOK TIME: 15 MINUTES • TOTAL: 20 MINUTES
SERVES: 4

Ingredients
Pork:
1-2 tbsp. Dijon mustard
3-4 strips of bacon
1 pork tenderloin
Apple Gravy:
½ - 1 tsp. Dijon mustard
1 tbsp. almond flour
2 tbsp. ghee
1 chopped onion
2-3 Granny Smith apples
1 C. vegetable broth

Directions:
1. **Preparing the Ingredients.** Spread Dijon mustard all over tenderloin and wrap the meat with strips of bacon.
2. **Air Frying**. Place into the Air fryer oven, set temperature to 360°F, and set time to 15 minutes and cook 10-15 minutes at 360 degrees. Use a meat thermometer to check for doneness.
   To make sauce, heat ghee in a pan and add shallots. Cook 1-2 minutes.
   Then add apples, cooking 3-5 minutes until softened.
   Add flour and ghee to make a roux. Add broth and mustard, stirring well to combine.
   When the sauce starts to bubble, add 1 cup of sautéed apples, cooking till sauce thickens.
   Once pork tenderloin I cook, allow to sit 5-10 minutes to rest before slicing.
   Serve topped with apple gravy.

PER SERVING: CALORIES: 552; FAT: 25G; PROTEIN:29G; SUGAR:6G

Dijon Garlic Pork Tenderloin

PREP: 5 MINUTES • COOK TIME: 10 MINUTES • TOTAL: 15 MINUTES
SERVES: 6

Ingredients
1 C. breadcrumbs
Pinch of cayenne pepper
3 crushed garlic cloves
2 tbsp. ground ginger
2 tbsp. Dijon mustard
2 tbsp. raw honey
4 tbsp. water
2 tsp. salt
1 pound pork tenderloin, sliced into 1-inch rounds

Directions:

1. **Preparing the Ingredients.** With pepper and salt, season all sides of tenderloin. Combine cayenne pepper, garlic, ginger, mustard, honey, and water until smooth. Dip pork rounds into the honey mixture and then into breadcrumbs, ensuring they all get coated well.
Place coated pork rounds into your Air fryer oven.
2. **Air Frying**. Set temperature to 400°F, and set time to 10 minutes. Cook 10 minutes at 400 degrees. Flip and then cook an additional 5 minutes until golden in color.

PER SERVING: CALORIES: 423; FAT: 18G; PROTEIN:31G; SUGAR:3G

Pork Neck with Salad

PREP: 10 MINUTES • **COOK TIME:** 12 MINUTES • **TOTAL:** 22 MINUTES
SERVES: 2

Ingredients

For Pork:
1 tablespoon soy sauce
1 tablespoon fish sauce
½ tablespoon oyster sauce
½ pound pork neck

For Salad:
1 ripe tomato, sliced tickly
8-10 Thai shallots, sliced
1 scallion, chopped
1 bunch fresh basil leaves
1 bunch fresh cilantro leaves

For Dressing:
3 tablespoons fish sauce
2 tablespoons olive oil
1 teaspoon apple cider vinegar
1 tablespoon palm sugar
2 bird eye chili
1 tablespoon garlic, minced

Directions:

1. **Preparing the Ingredients.** For pork in a bowl, mix together all ingredients except pork. Add pork neck and coat with marinade evenly. Refrigerate for about 2-3 hours. Preheat the Air fryer oven to 340 degrees F.
2. **Air Frying.** Place the pork neck onto a grill pan. Cook for about 12 minutes. Meanwhile, in a large salad bowl, mix together all salad ingredients. In a bowl, add all dressing ingredients and beat till well combined. Remove pork neck from Air fryer and cut into desired slices. Place pork slices over salad.

Chinese Braised Pork Belly

PREP: 5 MINUTES • COOK TIME: 20 MINUTES • TOTAL: 25 MINUTES
SERVES: 8

Ingredients
1 lb Pork Belly, sliced
1 Tbsp Oyster Sauce
1 Tbsp Sugar
2 Red Fermented Bean Curds
1 Tbsp Red Fermented Bean Curd Paste
1 Tbsp Cooking Wine
1/2 Tbsp Soy Sauce
1 Tsp Sesame Oil
1 Cup All Purpose Flour

Directions:
1. **Preparing the Ingredients.** Preheat the Air fryer oven to 390 degrees.
   In a small bowl, mix all ingredients together and rub the pork thoroughly with this mixture
   Set aside to marinate for at least 30 minutes or preferably overnight for the flavors to permeate the meat
   Coat each marinated pork belly slice in flour and place in the Air fryer oven tray
2. **Air Frying.** Cook for 15 to 20 minutes until crispy and tender.

Air Fryer Sweet and Sour Pork

PREP: 10 MINUTES • COOK TIME: 12 MINUTES • TOTAL: 22 MINUTES
SERVES: 6

Ingredients
3 tbsp. olive oil
1/16 tsp. Chinese Five Spice
¼ tsp. pepper
½ tsp. sea salt
1 tsp. pure sesame oil
2 eggs
1 C. almond flour
2 pounds pork, sliced into chunks

Sweet and Sour Sauce:
¼ tsp. sea salt
½ tsp. garlic powder
1 tbsp. low-sodium soy sauce
½ C. rice vinegar
5 tbsp. tomato paste
1/8 tsp. water
½ C. sweetener of choice

Directions:

1. **Preparing the Ingredients.** To make the dipping sauce, whisk all sauce ingredients together over medium heat, stirring 5 minutes. Simmer uncovered 5 minutes till thickened.
   Meanwhile, combine almond flour, five spice, pepper, and salt.
   In another bowl, mix eggs with sesame oil.
   Dredge pork in flour mixture and then in egg mixture. Shake any excess off before adding to air fryer rack/basket.
2. **Air Frying.** Set temperature to 340°F, and set time to 12 minutes.
   Serve with sweet and sour dipping sauce!

PER SERVING: CALORIES: 371; FAT: 17G; PROTEIN:27G; SUGAR:1G

Fried Pork Scotch Egg

PREP: 10 MINUTES • COOK TIME: 25 MINUTES • TOTAL: 35 MINUTES
SERVES: 2

Ingredients

3 soft-boiled eggs, peeled
8 ounces of raw minced pork, or sausage outside the casings
2 teaspoons of ground rosemary
2 teaspoons of garlic powder
Pinch of salt and pepper
2 raw eggs
1 cup of breadcrumbs (Panko, but other brands are fine, or home-made bread crumbs work too)

Directions:

1. **Preparing the Ingredients.** Cover the basket of the Air fryer oven with a lining of tin foil, leaving the edges uncovered to allow air to circulate through the basket. Preheat the air fryer to 350 degrees.
   In a mixing bowl, combine the raw pork with the rosemary, garlic powder, salt, and pepper. This will probably be easiest to do with your masher or bare hands (though make sure to wash thoroughly after handling raw meat!); combine until all the spices are evenly spread throughout the meat.
   Divide the meat mixture into three equal portions in the mixing bowl, and form each into balls with your hands.
   Lay a large sheet of plastic wrap on the countertop, and flatten one of the balls of meat on top of it, to form a wide, flat meat-circle.
   Place one of the peeled soft-boiled eggs in the center of the meat-circle and then, using the ends of the plastic wrap, pull the meat-circle so that it is fully covering and surrounding the soft-boiled egg.
   Tighten and shape the plastic wrap covering the meat so that if forms a ball, and make sure not to squeeze too hard lest you squish the soft-boiled egg at the center of the ball! Set aside.
   Repeat steps 5-7 with the other two soft-boiled eggs and portions of meat-mixture.
   In a separate mixing bowl, beat the two raw eggs until fluffy and until the yolks and whites are fully combined.
   One by one, remove the plastic wrap and dunk the pork-covered balls into the raw egg, and then roll them in the bread crumbs, covering fully and generously.

Place each of the bread-crumb covered meat-wrapped balls onto the foil-lined surface of the air fryer. Three of them should fit nicely, without touching.
2. **Air Frying.** Set the Air fryer oven timer to 25 minutes.
About halfway through the cooking time, shake the handle of the air-fryer vigorously, so that the scotch eggs inside roll around and ensure full coverage.
After 25 minutes, the air fryer will shut off, and the scotch eggs should be perfect – the meat fully cooked, the egg-yolks still runny on the inside, and the outsides crispy and golden-brown. Using tongs, place them on serving plates, slice in half, and enjoy

Juicy Pork Ribs Ole

PREP: 10 MINUTES • COOK TIME: 25 MINUTES • TOTAL: 35 MINUTES
SERVES: 4

Ingredients
1 rack of pork ribs
1/2 cup low-fat milk
1 tablespoon envelope taco seasoning mix
1 can tomato sauce
1/2 teaspoon ground black pepper
1 teaspoon seasoned salt
1 tablespoon cornstarch
1 teaspoon canola oil

Directions:
1. **Preparing the Ingredients.** Place all ingredients in a mixing dish; let them marinate for 1 hour.
2. **Air Frying**. Cook the marinated ribs approximately 25 minutes at 390 degrees F Work with batches. Enjoy .

Teriyaki Pork Rolls

PREP: 10 MINUTES • COOK TIME: 8 MINUTES • TOTAL: 20 MINUTES
SERVES: 6

Ingredients
1 tsp. almond flour
4 tbsp. low-sodium soy sauce
4 tbsp. mirin
4 tbsp. brown sugar
Thumb-sized amount of ginger, chopped
Pork belly slices
Enoki mushrooms

Directions:
1. **Preparing the Ingredients.** Mix brown sugar, mirin, soy sauce, almond flour, and ginger together until brown sugar dissolves.
   Take pork belly slices and wrap around a bundle of mushrooms. Brush each roll with teriyaki sauce. Chill half an hour.
   Preheat your Air fryer oven to 350 degrees and add marinated pork rolls.
2. **Air Frying.** Set temperature to 350°F, and set time to 8 minutes.

PER SERVING: CALORIES: 412; FAT: 9G; PROTEIN:19G; SUGAR:4G

Beef Recipes

Spicy Thai Beef Stir-Fry

PREP: 15 MINUTES • COOK TIME: 9 MINUTES • TOTAL: 24 MINUTES
SERVES: 4

Ingredients
1 pound sirloin steaks, thinly sliced
2 tablespoons lime juice, divided
⅓ cup crunchy peanut butter
½ cup beef broth
1 tablespoon olive oil
1½ cups broccoli florets
2 cloves garlic, sliced
1 to 2 red chile peppers, sliced

Directions:
1. **Preparing the Ingredients.** In a medium bowl, combine the steak with 1 tablespoon of the lime juice. Set aside.
   Combine the peanut butter and beef broth in a small bowl and mix well. Drain the beef and add the juice from the bowl into the peanut butter mixture.
   In a 6-inch metal bowl, combine the olive oil, steak, and broccoli.
2. **Air Frying.** Cook for 3 to 4 minutes or until the steak is almost cooked and the broccoli is crisp and tender, shaking the basket once during cooking time.
   Add the garlic, chile peppers, and the peanut butter mixture and stir.
   Cook for 3 to 5 minutes or until the sauce is bubbling and the broccoli is tender.
   Serve over hot rice.

PER SERVING: CALORIES: 387; FAT: 22G; PROTEIN:42G; FIBER:2G

Copycat Taco Bell Crunch Wraps

PREP: 10 MINUTES • COOK TIME: 2 MINUTES • TOTAL: 15 MINUTES
SERVES: 6

Ingredients
6 wheat tostadas
2 C. sour cream
2 C. Mexican blend cheese
2 C. shredded lettuce
12 ounces low-sodium nacho cheese
3 Roma tomatoes
6 12-inch wheat tortillas
1 1/3 C. water
2 packets low-sodium taco seasoning
2 pounds of lean ground beef

Directions:
1. **Preparing the Ingredients.** Ensure your air fryer is preheated to 400 degrees.
   Make beef according to taco seasoning packets.
   Place 2/3 C. prepared beef, 4 tbsp. cheese, 1 tostada, 1/3 C. sour cream, 1/3 C. lettuce, 1/6th of tomatoes and 1/3 C. cheese on each tortilla.
   Fold up tortillas edges and repeat with remaining ingredients.
   Lay the folded sides of tortillas down into the air fryer and spray with olive oil.
2. **Air Frying.** Set temperature to 400°F, and set time to 2 minutes. Cook 2 minutes till browned.

PER SERVING: CALORIES: 311; FAT: 9G; PROTEIN:22G; SUGAR:2

Meat Lovers' Pizza

PREP: 10 MINUTES • COOK TIME: 12 MINUTES • TOTAL: 22 MINUTES
SERVES: 2

Ingredients
1 pre-prepared 7-inch pizza pie crust, defrosted if necessary.
1/3 cup of marinara sauce.
2 ounces of grilled steak, sliced into bite-sized pieces
2 ounces of salami, sliced fine
2 ounces of pepperoni, sliced fine
¼ cup of American cheese
¼ cup of shredded mozzarella cheese

Directions:

1. **Preparing the Ingredients.** Preheat the Air fryer oven to 350 degrees. Lay the pizza dough flat on a sheet of parchment paper or tin foil, cut large enough to hold the entire pie crust, but small enough that it will leave the edges of theair frying rack/basket uncovered to allow for air circulation. Using a fork, stab the pizza dough several times across the surface – piercing the pie crust will allow air to circulate throughout the crust and ensure even cooking. With a deep soup spoon, ladle the marinara sauce onto the pizza dough, and spread evenly in expanding circles over the surface of the pie-crust. Be sure to leave at least ½ inch of bare dough around the edges, to ensure that extra-crispy crunchy first bite of the crust! Distribute the pieces of steak and the slices of salami and pepperoni evenly over the sauce-covered dough, then sprinkle the cheese in an even layer on top.

2. **Air Frying.** Set the Air fryer oven timer to 12 minutes, and place the pizza with foil or paper on the fryer's basket surface. Again, be sure to leave the edges of the basket uncovered to allow for proper air circulation, and don't let your bare fingers touch the hot surface. After 12 minutes, when the Air fryer oven shuts off, the cheese should be perfectly melted and lightly crisped, and the pie crust should be golden brown. Using a spatula – or two, if necessary, remove the pizza from the Oven rack/basket and set on a serving plate. Wait a few minutes until the pie is cool enough to handle, then cut into slices and serve.

Country Fried Steak

PREP: 5 MINUTES • COOK TIME: 12 MINUTES • TOTAL: 20 MINUTES
SERVES: 2

Ingredients
1 tsp. pepper
2 C. almond milk
2 tbsp. almond flour
6 ounces ground sausage meat
1 tsp. pepper
1 tsp. salt
1 tsp. garlic powder
1 tsp. onion powder
1 C. panko breadcrumbs
1 C. almond flour
3 beaten eggs
6 ounces sirloin steak, pounded till thin

Directions:
1. **Preparing the Ingredients.** Season panko breadcrumbs with spices. Dredge steak in flour, then egg, and then seasoned panko mixture. Place into air fryer rack/basket.
2. **Air Frying.** Set temperature to 370°F, and set time to 12 minutes.
   To make sausage gravy, cook sausage and drain off fat, but reserve 2 tablespoons. Add flour to sausage and mix until incorporated. Gradually mix in milk over medium to high heat till it becomes thick.
   Season mixture with pepper and cook 3 minutes longer.
   Serve steak topped with gravy and enjoy!

PER SERVING: CALORIES: 395; FAT: 11G; PROTEIN:39G; SUGAR:5G

Beef & veggie Spring Rolls

PREP: 5 MINUTES • COOK TIME: 12 MINUTES • TOTAL: 55 MINUTES
SERVES: 10

Ingredients
2-ounce Asian rice noodles
1 tablespoon sesame oil
7-ounce ground beef
1 small onion, chopped
3 garlic cloves, crushed
1 cup fresh mixed vegetables
1 teaspoon soy sauce
1 packet spring roll skins
2 tablespoons water
Olive oil, as required

Directions:

1. **Preparing the Ingredients.** Soak the noodles in warm water till soft. Drain and cut into small lengths. In a pan heat the oil and add the onion and garlic and sauté for about 4-5 minutes.
   Add beef and cook for about 4-5 minutes.
   Add vegetables and cook for about 5-7 minutes or till cooked through.
   Stir in soy sauce and remove from the heat.
   Immediately, stir in the noodles and keep aside till all the juices have been absorbed.
   Preheat the Air fryer oven to 350 degrees F. and preheat the oven to 350 degrees F also.
   Place the spring rolls skin onto a smooth surface.
   Add a line of the filling diagonally across.
   Fold the top point over the filling and then fold in both sides.
   On the final point, brush it with water before rolling to seal.
   Brush the spring rolls with oil.

2. **Air Frying.** Arrange the rolls in batches in the Air fryer oven and Cook for about 8 minutes.
   Repeat with remaining rolls.
   Now, place spring rolls onto a baking sheet.
   Bake for about 6 minutes per side

Air Fryer Roast Beef

PREP: 5 MINUTES • COOK TIME: 45 MINUTES • TOTAL: 50 MINUTES
SERVES: 6

Ingredients
Roast beef
1 tbsp. olive oil
Seasonings of choice

Directions:
1. **Preparing the Ingredients.** Ensure your air fryer is preheated to 160 degrees. Place roast in bowl and toss with olive oil and desired seasonings. Put seasoned roast into the Air fryer oven.
2. **Air Frying.** Set temperature to 160°F, and set time to 30 minutes and cook 30 minutes. Turn roast when the timer sounds and cook another 15 minutes.

PER SERVING: CALORIES: 267; FAT: 8G; PROTEIN:2G

Crispy Mongolian Beef

PREP: 5 MINUTES • COOK TIME: 10 MINUTES • TOTAL: 15 MINUTES
SERVES: 6

Ingredients
Olive oil
½ C. almond flour
2 pounds beef tenderloin or beef chuck, sliced into strips
Sauce:
½ C. chopped green onion
1 tsp. red chili flakes
1 tsp. almond flour
½ C. brown sugar
1 tsp. hoisin sauce
½ C. water
½ C. rice vinegar
½ C. low-sodium soy sauce
1 tbsp. chopped garlic
1 tbsp. finely chopped ginger
2 tbsp. olive oil

Directions:
1. **Preparing the Ingredients.** Toss strips of beef in almond flour, ensuring they are coated well. Add to the Air fryer oven.
2. **Air Frying.** Set temperature to 300°F, and set time to 10 minutes, and cook 10 minutes at 300 degrees.
   Meanwhile, add all sauce ingredients to the pan and bring to a boil. Mix well.
   Add beef strips to the sauce and cook 2 minutes.
   Serve over cauliflower rice!

PER SERVING: CALORIES: 290; FAT: 14G; PROTEIN:22G; SUGAR:1G

Swedish Meatballs

PREP: 10 MINUTES • COOK TIME: 14 MINUTES • TOTAL: 24 MINUTES
SERVES: 4

Ingredients
For the meatballs
1 pound 93% lean ground beef
1 (1-ounce) packet Lipton Onion Recipe Soup & Dip Mix
⅓ cup bread crumbs
1 egg, beaten
Salt
Pepper
For the gravy
1 cup beef broth
⅓ cup heavy cream
1 tablespoons all-purpose flour

Directions:

1. **Preparing the Ingredients.** In a large bowl, combine the ground beef, onion soup mix, bread crumbs, egg, and salt and pepper to taste. Mix thoroughly.
   Using 2 tablespoons of the meat mixture, create each meatball by rolling the beef mixture around in your hands. This should yield about 10 meatballs.
2. **Air Frying**. Place the meatballs in the Air fryer oven. It is okay to stack them. Cook for 14 minutes.
   While the meatballs cook, prepare the gravy. Heat a saucepan over medium-high heat. Add the beef broth and heavy cream. Stir for 1 to 2 minutes.
   Add the flour and stir. Cover and allow the sauce to simmer for 3 to 4 minutes, or until thick.
   Drizzle the gravy over the meatballs and serve.

PER SERVING: CALORIES: 178; FAT: 14G; PROTEIN:9G; FIBER:0

Tender Beef with Sour Cream Sauce

PREP: 5 MINUTES • COOK TIME: 12 MINUTES • TOTAL: 17 MINUTES
SERVES: 2

Ingredients
9 ounces tender beef, chopped
1 cup scallions, chopped
2 cloves garlic, smashed
3/4 cup sour cream
3/4 teaspoon salt
1/4 teaspoon black pepper, or to taste
1/2 teaspoon dried dill weed

Directions:
1. **Preparing the Ingredients.** Add the beef, scallions, and garlic to the baking dish.
2. **Air Frying.** Cook for about 5 minutes at 390 degrees F.
   Once the meat is starting to tender, pour in the sour cream. Stir in the salt, black pepper, and dill.
   Now, cook 7 minutes longer.

Air Fryer Burgers

PREP: 5 MINUTES • COOK TIME: 10 MINUTES • TOTAL: 15 MINUTES
SERVES: 4

Ingredients
1 pound lean ground beef
1 tsp. dried parsley
½ tsp. dried oregano
½ tsp. pepper
½ tsp. salt
½ tsp. onion powder
½ tsp. garlic powder
Few drops of liquid smoke
1 tsp. Worcestershire sauce

Directions:
1. **Preparing the Ingredients.** Ensure your air fryer is preheated to 350 degrees.
   Mix all seasonings together till combined.
   Place beef in a bowl and add seasonings. Mix well, but do not overmix.
   Make 4 patties from the mixture and using your thumb, making an indent in the center of each patty.
   Add patties to air fryer rack/basket.
2. **Air Frying.** Set temperature to 350°F, and set time to 10 minutes, and cook 10 minutes. No need to turn.

PER SERVING: CALORIES: 148; FAT: 5G; PROTEIN:24G; SUGAR:1G

Carrot and Beef Cocktail Balls

PREP: 5 MINUTES • COOK TIME: 20 MINUTES • TOTAL: 25 MINUTES
SERVES: 10

Ingredients
1 pound ground beef
2 carrots
1 red onion, peeled and chopped
2 cloves garlic
1/2 teaspoon dried rosemary, crushed
1/2 teaspoon dried basil
1 teaspoon dried oregano
1 egg
3/4 cup breadcrumbs
1/2 teaspoon salt
1/2 teaspoon black pepper, or to taste
1 cup plain flour

Directions:
1 **Preparing the Ingredients**. Place ground beef in a large bowl. In a food processor, pulse the carrot, onion, and garlic; transfer the vegetable mixture to a large-sized bowl.
Then, add the rosemary, basil, oregano, egg, breadcrumbs, salt, and black pepper.
Shape the mixture into even balls; refrigerate for about 30 minutes. Roll the balls into the flour.
2 **Air Frying**. Then, air-fry the balls at 350 degrees F for about 20 minutes, turning occasionally; work with batches. Serve with toothpicks.

Beef Steaks with Beans

PREP: 5 MINUTES • COOK TIME: 10 MINUTES • TOTAL: 15 MINUTES
SERVES: 4

Ingredients

4 beef steaks, trim the fat and cut into strips
1 cup green onions, chopped
2 cloves garlic, minced
1 red bell pepper, seeded and thinly sliced
1 can tomatoes, crushed
1 can cannellini beans
3/4 cup beef broth
1/4 teaspoon dried basil
1/2 teaspoon cayenne pepper
1/2 teaspoon sea salt
1/4 teaspoon ground black pepper, or to taste

Directions:

1. **Preparing the Ingredients**. Add the steaks, green onions and garlic to the Oven rack/basket. Place the Rack on the middle-shelf of the Air fryer oven.
2. **Air Frying**. Cook at 390 degrees F for 10 minutes, working in batches. Stir in the remaining ingredients and cook for an additional 5 minutes.

Mushroom Meatloaf

PREP: 5 MINUTES • COOK TIME: 25 MINUTES • TOTAL: 30 MINUTES
SERVES: 4

Ingredients
14-ounce lean ground beef
1 chorizo sausage, chopped finely
1 small onion, chopped
1 garlic clove, minced
2 tablespoons fresh cilantro, chopped
3 tablespoons breadcrumbs
1 egg
Salt and freshly ground black pepper, to taste
2 tablespoons fresh mushrooms, sliced thinly
3 tablespoons olive oil

Directions:
1. **Preparing the Ingredients.** Preheat the Air fryer to 390 degrees F.
   In a large bowl, add all ingredients except mushrooms and mix till well combined.
   In a baking pan, place the beef mixture.
   With the back of spatula, smooth the surface.
   Top with mushroom slices and gently, press into the meatloaf.
   Drizzle with oil evenly.
2. **Air Frying.** Arrange the pan in the Oven rack/basket. Place the Rack on the middle-shelf of the Air fryer oven. Cook for about 25 minutes.
   Cut the meatloaf in desires size wedges and serve.

Seafood Recipes

Bacon Wrapped Shrimp
PREP: 5 MINUTES • COOK TIME: 5 MINUTES • TOTAL: 10 MINUTES
SERVES: 4

Ingredients
1¼ pound tiger shrimp, peeled and deveined
1 pound bacon

Directions:
1. **Preparing the Ingredients.** Wrap each shrimp with a slice of bacon. Refrigerate for about 20 minutes. Preheat the Air fryer oven to 390 degrees F.
2. **Air Frying.** Arrange the shrimp in the Oven rack/basket. Place the Rack on the middle-shelf of the Air fryer oven. Cook for about 5-7 minutes.

Crispy Paprika Fish Fillets

PREP: 5 MINUTES • COOK TIME: 15 MINUTES • TOTAL: 20 MINUTES
SERVES: 4

Ingredients
1/2 cup seasoned breadcrumbs
1 tablespoon balsamic vinegar
1/2 teaspoon seasoned salt
1 teaspoon paprika
1/2 teaspoon ground black pepper
1 teaspoon celery seed
2 fish fillets, halved
1 egg, beaten

Directions:
1. **Preparing the Ingredients.** Add the breadcrumbs, vinegar, salt, paprika, ground black pepper, and celery seeds to your food processor. Process for about 30 seconds.
Coat the fish fillets with the beaten egg; then, coat them with the breadcrumbs mixture.
2. **Air Frying.** Cook at 350 degrees F for about 15 minutes.

Air Fryer Salmon

PREP: 5 MINUTES • COOK TIME: 10 MINUTES • TOTAL: 15 MINUTES
SERVES: 2

Ingredients
½ tsp. salt
½ tsp. garlic powder
½ tsp. smoked paprika
Salmon

Directions:
1. **Preparing the Ingredients.** Mix spices and sprinkle onto salmon. Place seasoned salmon into the Air fryer oven.
2. **Air Frying.** Set temperature to 400°F, and set time to 10 minutes.

PER SERVING: CALORIES: 185; FAT: 11G; PROTEIN:21G; SUGAR:0G

Sweet And Savory Breaded Shrimp

PREP: 5 MINUTES • COOK TIME: 20 MINUTES • TOTAL: 25 MINUTES
SERVES: 2

Ingredients

½ pound of fresh shrimp, peeled from their shells and rinsed
2 raw eggs
½ cup of breadcrumbs (we like Panko, but any brand or home recipe will do)
½ white onion, peeled and rinsed and finely chopped
1 teaspoon of ginger-garlic paste
½ teaspoon of turmeric powder
½ teaspoon of red chili powder
½ teaspoon of cumin powder
½ teaspoon of black pepper powder
½ teaspoon of dry mango powder
Pinch of salt

Directions:

1. **Preparing the Ingredients.** Cover the basket of the Air fryer oven with a lining of tin foil, leaving the edges uncovered to allow air to circulate through the basket.
   Preheat the Air fryer oven to 350 degrees.
   In a large mixing bowl, beat the eggs until fluffy and until the yolks and whites are fully combined.
   Dunk all the shrimp in the egg mixture, fully submerging.
   In a separate mixing bowl, combine the bread crumbs with all the dry ingredients until evenly blended.
   One by one, coat the egg-covered shrimp in the mixed dry ingredients so that fully covered, and place on the foil-lined air-fryer basket.
2. **Air Frying.** Set the air-fryer timer to 20 minutes.
   Halfway through the cooking time, shake the handle of the air-fryer so that the breaded shrimp jostles inside and fry-coverage is even.
   After 20 minutes, when the fryer shuts off, the shrimp will be perfectly cooked and their breaded crust golden-brown and delicious! Using tongs, remove from the air fryer and set on a serving dish to cool.

Quick Paella

PREP: 7 MINUTES • COOK TIME: 15 MINUTES • TOTAL: 22 MINUTES
SERVES: 4

Ingredients

1 (10-ounce) package frozen cooked rice, thawed
1 (6-ounce) jar artichoke hearts, drained and chopped
¼ cup vegetable broth
½ teaspoon turmeric
½ teaspoon dried thyme
1 cup frozen cooked small shrimp
½ cup frozen baby peas
1 tomato, diced

Directions:

1. **Preparing the Ingredients.** In a 6-by-6-by-2-inch pan, combine the rice, artichoke hearts, vegetable broth, turmeric, and thyme, and stir gently.

2. **Air Frying.** Place in the Air fryer oven and bake for 8 to 9 minutes or until the rice is hot. Remove from the air fryer and gently stir in the shrimp, peas, and tomato. Cook for 5 to 8 minutes or until the shrimp and peas are hot and the paella is bubbling.

PER SERVING: CALORIES: 345; FAT: 1G; PROTEIN:18G; FIBER:4G

Coconut Shrimp

PREP: 15 MINUTES • COOK TIME: 5 MINUTES • TOTAL: 20 MINUTES
SERVES: 4

Ingredients
1 (8-ounce) can crushed pineapple
½ cup sour cream
¼ cup pineapple preserves
2 egg whites
⅔ cup cornstarch
⅔ cup sweetened coconut
1 cup panko bread crumbs
1 pound uncooked large shrimp, thawed if frozen, deveined and shelled
Olive oil for misting

Directions:

1. **Preparing the Ingredients.** Drain the crushed pineapple well, reserving the juice. In a small bowl, combine the pineapple, sour cream, and preserves, and mix well. Set aside. In a shallow bowl, beat the egg whites with 2 tablespoons of the reserved pineapple liquid. Place the cornstarch on a plate. Combine the coconut and bread crumbs on another plate. Dip the shrimp into the cornstarch, shake it off, then dip into the egg white mixture and finally into the coconut mixture. Place the shrimp in the air fryer rack/basket and mist with oil.

2. **Air Frying.** Air-fry for 5 to 7 minutes or until the shrimp are crisp and golden brown.

PER SERVING: CALORIES: 524; FAT: 14G; PROTEIN:33G; FIBER:4G

Cilantro-Lime Fried Shrimp

PREP: 10 MINUTES • COOK TIME: 10 MINUTES • TOTAL: 20 MINUTES
SERVES: 4

Ingredients

1 pound raw shrimp, peeled and deveined with tails on or off (see Prep tip)
½ cup chopped fresh cilantro
Juice of 1 lime
1 egg
½ cup all-purpose flour
¾ cup bread crumbs
Salt
Pepper
Cooking oil
½ cup cocktail sauce (optional)

Directions:

1. **Preparing the Ingredients.** Place the shrimp in a plastic bag and add the cilantro and lime juice. Seal the bag. Shake to combine. Marinate in the refrigerator for 30 minutes.
In a small bowl, beat the egg. In another small bowl, place the flour. Place the bread crumbs in a third small bowl, and season with salt and pepper to taste.
Spray the air fryer rack/basket with cooking oil.
Remove the shrimp from the plastic bag. Dip each in the flour, then the egg, and then the bread crumbs.
2. **Air Frying.** Place the shrimp in the Air fryer oven. It is okay to stack them. Spray the shrimp with cooking oil. Cook for 4 minutes.
Open the air fryer and flip the shrimp. I recommend flipping individually instead of shaking to keep the breading intact. Cook for an additional 4 minutes, or until crisp.
Cool before serving. Serve with cocktail sauce if desired.

PER SERVING: CALORIES: 254; FAT:4G; PROTEIN:29G; FIBER:1G

Lemony Tuna

PREP: 10 MINUTES • COOK TIME: 10 MINUTES • TOTAL: 20 MINUTES
SERVES: 4

Ingredients
2 (6-ounce) cans water packed plain tuna
2 teaspoons Dijon mustard
½ cup breadcrumbs
1 tablespoon fresh lime juice
2 tablespoons fresh parsley, chopped
1 egg
Chefman of hot sauce
3 tablespoons canola oil
Salt and freshly ground black pepper, to taste

Directions:
1. **Preparing the Ingredients.** Drain most of the liquid from the canned tuna. In a bowl, add the fish, mustard, crumbs, citrus juice, parsley, and hot sauce and mix till well combined. Add a little canola oil if it seems too dry. Add egg, salt and stir to combine. Make the patties from tuna mixture. Refrigerate the tuna patties for about 2 hours.
2. **Air Frying.** Preheat the air fryer to 355 degrees F. Cook for about 10-12 minutes.

Grilled Soy Salmon Fillets

PREP: 5 MINUTES • COOK TIME: 8 MINUTES • TOTAL: 13 MINUTES
SERVES: 4

Ingredients
4 salmon fillets
1/4 teaspoon ground black pepper
1/2 teaspoon cayenne pepper
1/2 teaspoon salt
1 teaspoon onion powder
1 tablespoon fresh lemon juice
1/2 cup soy sauce
1/2 cup water
1 tablespoon honey
2 tablespoons extra-virgin olive oil

Directions:
1 **Preparing the Ingredients.** Firstly, pat the salmon fillets dry using kitchen towels. Season the salmon with black pepper, cayenne pepper, salt, and onion powder.
To make the marinade, combine together the lemon juice, soy sauce, water, honey, and olive oil. Marinate the salmon for at least 2 hours in your refrigerator.
Arrange the fish fillets on a grill basket in your Air fryer oven.
2 **Air Frying**. Bake at 330 degrees for 8 to 9 minutes, or until salmon fillets are easily flaked with a fork.
Work with batches and serve warm.

Old Bay Crab Cakes

PREP: 10 MINUTES • COOK TIME: 20 MINUTES • TOTAL: 30 MINUTES
SERVES: 4

Ingredients

2 slices dried bread, crusts removed
Small amount of milk
1 tablespoon mayonnaise
1 tablespoon Worcestershire sauce
1 tablespoon baking powder
1 tablespoon parsley flakes
1 teaspoon Old Bay® Seasoning
1/4 teaspoon salt
1 egg
1 pound lump crabmeat

Directions:

1. **Preparing the Ingredients.** Crush your bread over a large bowl until it is broken down into small pieces. Add milk and stir until bread crumbs are moistened. Mix in mayo and Worcestershire sauce. Add remaining ingredients and mix well. Shape into 4 patties.
2. **Air Frying.** Cook at 360 degrees for 20 minutes, flip half way through.

PER SERVING: CALORIES: 165; CARBS:5.8; FAT: 4.5G; PROTEIN:24G; FIBER:0G

Scallops and Spring Veggies

PREP: 10 MINUTES • COOK TIME: 8 MINUTES • TOTAL: 18 MINUTES
SERVES: 4

Ingredients
½ pound asparagus ends trimmed, cut into 2-inch pieces
1 cup sugar snap peas
1 pound sea scallops
1 tablespoon lemon juice
2 teaspoons olive oil
½ teaspoon dried thyme
Pinch salt
Freshly ground black pepper

Directions:
1. **Preparing the Ingredients.** Place the asparagus and sugar snap peas in the Oven rack/basket. Place the Rack on the middle-shelf of the Air fryer oven.
2. **Air Frying.** Cook for 2 to 3 minutes or until the vegetables are just starting to get tender. Meanwhile, check the scallops for a small muscle attached to the side, and pull it off and discard.
   In a medium bowl, toss the scallops with the lemon juice, olive oil, thyme, salt, and pepper. Place into the Oven rack/basket on top of the vegetables. Place the Rack on the middle-shelf of the Air fryer oven.
3. **Air Frying.** Steam for 5 to 7 minutes. Until the scallops are just firm, and the vegetables are tender. Serve immediately.

PER SERVING: CALORIES: 162; CARBS:10G; FAT: 4G; PROTEIN:22G; FIBER:3G

Fried Calamari

PREP: 8 MINUTES • COOK TIME: 7 MINUTES • TOTAL: 15 MINUTES
SERVES: 6-8

Ingredients
½ tsp. salt
½ tsp. Old Bay seasoning
1/3 C. plain cornmeal
½ C. semolina flour
½ C. almond flour
5-6 C. olive oil
1 ½ pounds baby squid

Directions:
1. **Preparing the Ingredients.** Rinse squid in cold water and slice tentacles, keeping just ¼-inch of the hood in one piece.
   Combine 1-2 pinches of pepper, salt, Old Bay seasoning, cornmeal, and both flours together. Dredge squid pieces into flour mixture and place into the Air fryer oven.
2. **Air Frying.** Spray liberally with olive oil. Cook 15 minutes at 345 degrees till coating turns a golden brown.

PER SERVING: CALORIES: 211; CARBS:55; FAT: 6G; PROTEIN:21G; SUGAR:1G

Soy and Ginger Shrimp

PREP: 8 MINUTES • COOK TIME: 10 MINUTES • TOTAL: 15 MINUTES
SERVES: 4

Ingredients
2 tablespoons olive oil
2 tablespoons scallions, finely chopped
2 cloves garlic, chopped
1 teaspoon fresh ginger, grated
1 tablespoon dry white wine
1 tablespoon balsamic vinegar
1/4 cup soy sauce
1 tablespoon sugar
1 pound shrimp
Salt and ground black pepper, to taste

Directions:
1. **Preparing the Ingredients.** To make the marinade, warm the oil in a saucepan; cook all ingredients, except the shrimp, salt, and black pepper. Now, let it cool.
Marinate the shrimp, covered, at least an hour, in the refrigerator.
2. **Air Frying.** After that, bake the shrimp at 350 degrees F for 8 to 10 minutes (depending on the size), turning once or twice. Season prepared shrimp with salt and black pepper and serve right away.

Crispy Cheesy Fish Fingers

PREP: 10 MINUTES • COOK TIME: 20 MINUTES • TOTAL: 30 MINUTES
SERVES: 4

Ingredients

Large codfish filet, approximately 6-8 ounces, fresh or frozen and thawed, cut into 1 ½-inch strips
2 raw eggs
½ cup of breadcrumbs (we like Panko, but any brand or home recipe will do)
2 tablespoons of shredded or powdered parmesan cheese
1 tablespoons of shredded cheddar cheese
Pinch of salt and pepper

Directions:

1. **Preparing the Ingredients.** Cover the basket of the Air fryer oven with a lining of tin foil, leaving the edges uncovered to allow air to circulate through the basket.
   Preheat the air fryer to 350 degrees.
   In a large mixing bowl, beat the eggs until fluffy and until the yolks and whites are fully combined.
   Dunk all the fish strips in the beaten eggs, fully submerging.
   In a separate mixing bowl, combine the bread crumbs with the parmesan, cheddar, and salt and pepper, until evenly mixed.
   One by one, coat the egg-covered fish strips in the mixed dry ingredients so that they're fully covered, and place on the foil-lined Oven rack/basket. Place the Rack on the middle-shelf of the Air fryer oven.
2. **Air Frying.** Set the air-fryer timer to 20 minutes.
   Halfway through the cooking time, shake the handle of the air-fryer so that the breaded fish jostles inside and fry-coverage is even.
   After 20 minutes, when the fryer shuts off, the fish strips will be perfectly cooked and their breaded crust golden-brown and delicious! Using tongs, remove from the air fryer and set on a serving dish to cool.

Panko-Crusted Tilapia

PREP: 5 MINUTES • COOK TIME: 10 MINUTES • TOTAL: 15 MINUTES
SERVES: 3

Ingredients
2 tsp. Italian seasoning
2 tsp. lemon pepper
1/3 C. panko breadcrumbs
1/3 C. egg whites
1/3 C. almond flour
3 tilapia fillets
Olive oil

Directions:
1. **Preparing the Ingredients.** Place panko, egg whites, and flour into separate bowls. Mix lemon pepper and Italian seasoning in with breadcrumbs.
Pat tilapia fillets dry. Dredge in flour, then egg, then breadcrumb mixture.
2. **Air Frying.** Add to the Oven rack/basket and spray lightly with olive oil. Place the Rack on the middle-shelf of the Air fryer oven.
Cook 10-11 minutes at 400 degrees, making sure to flip halfway through cooking.

PER SERVING: CALORIES: 256; FAT: 9G; PROTEIN:39G; SUGAR:5G

Fish Cakes With Mango Relish

PREP: 5 MINUTES • COOK TIME: 10 MINUTES • TOTAL: 15 MINUTES
SERVES: 4

Ingredients
1 lb White Fish Fillets
3 Tbsps Ground Coconut
1 Ripened Mango
½ Tsps Chili Paste
Tbsps Fresh Parsley
1 Green Onion
1 Lime
1 Tsp Salt
1 Egg

Directions:

1. **Preparing the Ingredients.** To make the relish, peel and dice the mango into cubes. Combine with a half teaspoon of chili paste, a tablespoon of parsley, and the zest and juice of half a lime.
   In a food processor, pulse the fish until it forms a smooth texture. Place into a bowl and add the salt, egg, chopped green onion, parsley, two tablespoons of the coconut, and the remainder of the chili paste and lime zest and juice. Combine well
   Portion the mixture into 10 equal balls and flatten them into small patties. Pour the reserved tablespoon of coconut onto a dish and roll the patties over to coat.
   Preheat the Air Fryer to 390 degrees

2. **Air Frying.** Place the fish cakes into the Air fryer oven and cook for 8 minutes. They should be crisp and lightly browned when ready
   Serve hot with mango relish

Firecracker Shrimp

PREP: 10 MINUTES • COOK TIME: 8 MINUTES • TOTAL: 18 MINUTES
SERVES: 4

Ingredients

For the shrimp
1 pound raw shrimp, peeled and deveined
Salt
Pepper
1 egg
½ cup all-purpose flour
¾ cup panko bread crumbs
Cooking oil

For the firecracker sauce
⅓ cup sour cream
2 tablespoons Sriracha
¼ cup sweet chili sauce

Directions:

1. **Preparing the Ingredients.** Season the shrimp with salt and pepper to taste. In a small bowl, beat the egg. In another small bowl, place the flour. In a third small bowl, add the panko bread crumbs.
   Spray the Oven rack/basket with cooking oil. Dip the shrimp in the flour, then the egg, and then the bread crumbs. Place the shrimp in the Oven rack/basket. It is okay to stack them. Spray the shrimp with cooking oil. Place the Rack on the middle-shelf of the Air fryer oven.

2. **Air Frying.** Cook for 4 minutes. Open the Air fryer oven and flip the shrimp. I recommend flipping individually instead of shaking to keep the breading intact. Cook for an additional 4 minutes or until crisp.
   While the shrimp is cooking, make the firecracker sauce: In a small bowl, combine the sour cream, Sriracha, and sweet chili sauce. Mix well. Serve with the shrimp.

PER SERVING: CALORIES: 266; CARBS:23g; FAT:6G; PROTEIN:27G; FIBER:1G

Sesame Seeds Coated Fish

PREP: 10 MINUTES • COOK TIME: 8 MINUTES • TOTAL: 18 MINUTES
SERVES: 5

Ingredients
3 tablespoons plain flour
2 eggs
½ cup sesame seeds, toasted
½ cup breadcrumbs
1/8 teaspoon dried rosemary, crushed
Pinch of salt
Pinch of black pepper
3 tablespoons olive oil
5 frozen fish fillets (white fish of your choice)

Directions:

1. **Preparing the Ingredients.** In a shallow dish, place flour. In a second shallow dish, beat the eggs. In a third shallow dish, add remaining ingredients except fish fillets and mix till a crumbly mixture forms.
   Coat the fillets with flour and shake off the excess flour.
   Next, dip the fillets in the egg.
   Then coat the fillets with sesame seeds mixture generously.
   Preheat the Air fryer oven to 390 degrees F.
2. **Air Frying.** Line an Air fryer rack/basket with a piece of foil. Arrange the fillets into prepared basket.
   Cook for about 14 minutes, flipping once after 10 minutes.

Crispy Paprika Fish Fillets

PREP: 5 MINUTES • COOK TIME: 15 MINUTES • TOTAL: 20 MINUTES
SERVES: 4

Ingredients
1/2 cup seasoned breadcrumbs
1 tablespoon balsamic vinegar
1/2 teaspoon seasoned salt
1 teaspoon paprika
1/2 teaspoon ground black pepper
1 teaspoon celery seed
2 fish fillets, halved
1 egg, beaten

Directions:
1. **Preparing the Ingredients.** Add the breadcrumbs, vinegar, salt, paprika, ground black pepper, and celery seeds to your food processor. Process for about 30 seconds.
Coat the fish fillets with the beaten egg; then, coat them with the breadcrumbs mixture.
2. **Air Frying.** Cook at 350 degrees F for about 15 minutes.

Parmesan Shrimp

PREP: 5 MINUTES • COOK TIME: 10 MINUTES • TOTAL: 15 MINUTES
SERVES: 4

Ingredients
2 tbsp. olive oil
1 tsp. onion powder
1 tsp. basil
½ tsp. oregano
1 tsp. pepper
2/3 C. grated parmesan cheese
4 minced garlic cloves
pounds of jumbo cooked shrimp (peeled/deveined)

Directions:
1. **Preparing the Ingredients**. Mix all seasonings together and gently toss shrimp with the mixture.
2. **Air Frying.** Spray olive oil into the Oven rack/basket and add seasoned shrimp. Place the Rack on the middle-shelf of the Air fryer oven. Cook 8-10 minutes at 350 degrees. Squeeze lemon juice over shrimp right before devouring!

PER SERVING: CALORIES: 351; FAT:11G; PROTEIN:19G; SUGAR:1G

Fish and Chips

PREP: 10 MINUTES • COOK TIME: 20 MINUTES • TOTAL: 30 MINUTES
SERVES: 4

Ingredients
4 (4-ounce) fish fillets
Pinch salt
Freshly ground black pepper
½ teaspoon dried thyme
1 egg white
¾ cup crushed potato chips
2 tablespoons olive oil, divided
1 russet potatoes, peeled and cut into strips

Directions:
1. **Preparing the Ingredients.** Pat the fish fillets dry and sprinkle with salt, pepper, and thyme. Set aside.
   In a shallow bowl, beat the egg white until foamy. In another bowl, combine the potato chips and 1 tablespoon of olive oil and mix until combined.
   Dip the fish fillets into the egg white, then into the crushed potato chip mixture to coat.
   Toss the fresh potato strips with the remaining 1 tablespoon olive oil.
2. **Air Frying.** Use your separator to divide the Oven rack/basket in half, then fry the chips and fish. The chips will take about 20 minutes; the fish will take about 10 to 12 minutes to cook.

PER SERVING: CALORIES: 374; FAT:16G; PROTEIN:30G; FIBER:4G

Crab Cakes

PREP: 5 MINUTES • COOK TIME: 10 MINUTES • TOTAL: 15 MINUTES
SERVES: 4

Ingredients
8 ounces jumbo lump crabmeat
1 tablespoon Old Bay Seasoning
⅓ cup bread crumbs
¼ cup diced red bell pepper
¼ cup diced green bell pepper
1 egg
¼ cup mayonnaise
Juice of ½ lemon
1 teaspoon flour
Cooking oil

Directions:
1 **Preparing the Ingredients.** In a large bowl, combine the crabmeat, Old Bay Seasoning, bread crumbs, red bell pepper, green bell pepper, egg, mayo, and lemon juice. Mix gently to combine.
Form the mixture into 4 patties. Sprinkle ¼ teaspoon of flour on top of each patty.
2 **Air Frying.** Place the crab cakes in the Air fryer oven. Spray them with cooking oil. Cook for 10 minutes.
Serve.

Sweet Recipes

Fried Peaches
PREP: 2 HOURS 10 MINUTES • COOK TIME: 15 MINUTES • TOTAL: 15 MINUTES
SERVES: 4

Ingredients
4 ripe peaches (1/2 a peach = 1 serving)
1 1/2 cups flour
Salt
2 egg yolks
3/4 cups cold water
1 1/2 tablespoons olive oil
2 tablespoons brandy
4 egg whites
Cinnamon/sugar mix

Directions:
1. **Preparing the Ingredients.** Mix flour, egg yolks, and salt in a mixing bowl. Slowly mix in water, then add brandy. Set the mixture aside for 2 hours and go do something for 1 hour 45 minutes.
   Boil a large pot of water and cut an X at the bottom of each peach. While the water boils, fill another large bowl with water and ice. Boil each peach for about a minute, then plunge it in the ice bath. Now the peels should basically fall off the peach. Beat the egg whites and mix into the batter mix. Dip each peach in the mix to coat.
2. **Air Frying.** Cook at 360 degrees for 10 Minutes.
   Prepare a plate with cinnamon/sugar mix, roll peaches in the mix and serve.

PER SERVING: CALORIES: 306; FAT:.3G; PROTEIN:10G; FIBER:2.7G

Apple Dumplings

PREP: 10 MINUTES • COOK TIME: 25 MINUTES • TOTAL: 35 MINUTES
SERVES: 4

Ingredients
2 tbsp. melted coconut oil
2 puff pastry sheets
1 tbsp. brown sugar
2 tbsp. raisins
2 small apples of choice

Directions:
1. **Preparing the Ingredients.** Ensure your air fryer is preheated to 356 degrees.
   Core and peel apples and mix with raisins and sugar.
   Place a bit of apple mixture into puff pastry sheets and brush sides with melted coconut oil.
2. **Air Frying.** Place into the Air fryer oven. Cook 25 minutes, turning halfway through. Will be golden when done.

PER SERVING: CALORIES: 367; FAT:7G; PROTEIN:2G; SUGAR:5G

Raspberry Cream Rol-Ups

PREP: 10 MINUTES • COOK TIME: 25 MINUTES • TOTAL: 35 MINUTES
SERVES: 4

Ingredients

1 cup of fresh raspberries rinsed and patted dry
½ cup of cream cheese softened to room temperature
¼ cup of brown sugar
¼ cup of sweetened condensed milk
1 egg
1 teaspoon of corn starch
6 spring roll wrappers (any brand will do, we like Blue Dragon or Tasty Joy, both available through Target or Walmart, or any large grocery chain)
¼ cup of water

Directions:

1. **Preparing the Ingredients.** Cover the basket of the Air fryer oven with a lining of tin foil, leaving the edges uncovered to allow air to circulate through the basket. Preheat the Air fryer oven to 350 degrees.

    In a mixing bowl, combine the cream cheese, brown sugar, condensed milk, cornstarch, and egg. Beat or whip thoroughly, until all ingredients are completely mixed and fluffy, thick and stiff.

    Spoon even amounts of the creamy filling into each spring roll wrapper, then top each dollop of filling with several raspberries.

    Roll up the wraps around the creamy raspberry filling, and seal the seams with a few dabs of water.

    Place each roll on the foil-lined Oven rack/basket, seams facing down. Place the Rack on the middle-shelf of the Air fryer oven.

2. **Air Frying.** Set the Air fryer oven timer to 10 minutes. During cooking, shake the handle of the fryer basket to ensure a nice even surface crisp.

    After 10 minutes, when the Air fryer oven shuts off, the spring rolls should be golden brown and perfect on the outside, while the raspberries and cream filling will have cooked together in a glorious fusion. Remove with tongs and serve hot or cold.

Air Fryer Chocolate Cake

PREP: 5 MINUTES • COOK TIME: 35 MINUTES • TOTAL: 40 MINUTES
SERVES: 8-10

Ingredients
- ½ C. hot water
- 1 tsp. vanilla
- ¼ C. olive oil
- ½ C. almond milk
- 1 egg
- ½ tsp. salt
- ¾ tsp. baking soda
- ¾ tsp. baking powder
- ½ C. unsweetened cocoa powder
- 2 C. almond flour
- 1 C. brown sugar

Directions:

1. **Preparing the Ingredients.** Preheat your air fryer to 356 degrees. Stir all dry ingredients together. Then stir in wet ingredients. Add hot water last. The batter will be thin, no worries.
2. **Air Frying.** Pour cake batter into a pan that fits into the fryer. Cover with foil and poke holes into the foil.
   Bake 35 minutes.
   Discard foil and then bake another 10 minutes.

PER SERVING: CALORIES: 378; FAT:9G; PROTEIN:4G; SUGAR:5G

Chocolate Donuts

PREP: 5 MINUTES • COOK TIME: 20 MINUTES • TOTAL: 25 MINUTES
SERVES: 8-10

Ingredients
(8-ounce) can jumbo biscuits
Cooking oil
Chocolate sauce, such as Hershey's

Directions:
1 **Preparing the Ingredients**. Separate the biscuit dough into 8 biscuits and place them on a flat work surface. Use a small circle cookie cutter or a biscuit cutter to cut a hole in the center of each biscuit. You can also cut the holes using a knife.
   Spray the Oven rack/basket with cooking oil. Place the Rack on the middle-shelf of the Air fryer oven.
2 **Air Frying.** Place 4 donuts in the air fryer. Do not stack. Spray with cooking oil. Cook for 4 minutes.
   Open the air fryer and flip the donuts. Cook for an additional 4 minutes.
   Remove the cooked donuts from the air fryer, then repeat steps 3 and 4 for the remaining 4 donuts.
   Drizzle chocolate sauce over the donuts and enjoy while warm.

PER SERVING: CALORIES: 181; FAT:98G; PROTEIN:3G; FIBER:1G

Fried Bananas with Chocolate Sauce

PREP: 10 MINUTES • COOK TIME: 10 MINUTES • TOTAL: 20 MINUTES
SERVES: 2

Ingredients
1 large egg
¼ cup cornstarch
¼ cup plain bread crumbs
3 bananas, halved crosswise
Cooking oil
Chocolate sauce (see Ingredient tip)

Directions:
1. **Preparing the Ingredients.** In a small bowl, beat the egg. In another bowl, place the cornstarch. Place the bread crumbs in a third bowl. Dip the bananas in the cornstarch, then the egg, and then the bread crumbs.
   Spray the air fryer rack/basket with cooking oil. Place the bananas in the basket and spray them with cooking oil.
2. **Air Frying.** Cook for 5 minutes. Open the air fryer and flip the bananas. Cook for an additional 2 minutes. Transfer the bananas to plates.
   Drizzle the chocolate sauce over the bananas, and serve.
   You can make your own chocolate sauce using 2 tablespoons milk and ¼ cup chocolate chips. Heat a saucepan over medium-high heat. Add the milk and stir for 1 to 2 minutes. Add the chocolate chips. Stir for 2 minutes, or until the chocolate has melted.

PER SERVING: CALORIES: 203; FAT:6G; PROTEIN:3G; FIBER:3G

Apple Hand Pies
PREP: 5 MINUTES • COOK TIME: 8 MINUTES • TOTAL: 13 MINUTES
SERVES: 6

Ingredients
15-ounces no-sugar-added apple pie filling
1 store-bought crust

Directions:
1. **Preparing the Ingredients.** Lay out pie crust and slice into equal-sized squares. Place 2 tbsp. filling into each square and seal crust with a fork.
2. **Air Frying.** Place into the Air fryer oven. Cook 8 minutes at 390 degrees until golden in color.

PER SERVING: CALORIES: 278; FAT:10G; PROTEIN:5G; SUGAR:4G

Chocolaty Banana Muffins

PREP: 5 MINUTES • COOK TIME: 25 MINUTES • TOTAL: 35 MINUTES
SERVES: 12

Ingredients

¾ cup whole wheat flour
¾ cup plain flour
¼ cup cocoa powder
¼ teaspoon baking powder
1 teaspoon baking soda
¼ teaspoon salt
2 large bananas, peeled and mashed
1 cup sugar
1/3 cup canola oil
1 egg
½ teaspoon vanilla essence
1 cup mini chocolate chips

Directions:

1. **Preparing the Ingredients.** In a large bowl, mix together flour, cocoa powder, baking powder, baking soda, and salt.
   In another bowl, add bananas, sugar, oil, egg and vanilla extract and beat till well combined.
   Slowly, add flour mixture in egg mixture and mix till just combined.
   Fold in chocolate chips.
   Preheat the Air Fryer to 345 degrees F. Grease 12 muffin molds.
2. **Air Frying.** Transfer the mixture into prepared muffin molds evenly and cook for about 20-25 minutes or till a toothpick inserted in the center comes out clean.
   Remove the muffin molds from Air fryer and keep on wire rack to cool for about 10 minutes. Carefully turn on a wire rack to cool completely before serving.

Blueberry Lemon Muffins

PREP: 5 MINUTES • COOK TIME: 10 MINUTES • TOTAL: 15 MINUTES
SERVES: 12

Ingredients
1 tsp. vanilla
Juice and zest of 1 lemon
2 eggs
1 C. blueberries
½ C. cream
¼ C. avocado oil
½ C. monk fruit
2 ½ C. almond flour

Directions:
1. **Preparing the Ingredients**. Mix monk fruit and flour together.
   In another bowl, mix vanilla, egg, lemon juice, and cream together. Add mixtures together and blend well.
   Spoon batter into cupcake holders.
2. **Air Frying**. Place in the Air fryer oven. Bake 10 minutes at 320 degrees, checking at 6 minutes to ensure you don't overbake them.

PER SERVING: CALORIES: 317; FAT:11G; PROTEIN:3G; SUGAR:5G

Sweet Cream Cheese Wontons

PREP: 5 MINUTES • COOK TIME: 5 MINUTES • TOTAL: 10 MINUTES
SERVES: 16

Ingredients
1 egg mixed with a bit of water
Wonton wrappers
½ C. powdered erythritol
8 ounces softened cream cheese
Olive oil

Directions:
1. **Preparing the Ingredients.** Mix sweetener and cream cheese together.
   Lay out 4 wontons at a time and cover with a dish towel to prevent drying out.
   Place ½ of a teaspoon of cream cheese mixture into each wrapper.
   Dip finger into egg/water mixture and fold diagonally to form a triangle. Seal edges well.
   Repeat with remaining ingredients.
2. **Air Frying.** Place filled wontons into the Air fryer oven and cook 5 minutes at 400 degrees, shaking halfway through cooking.

PER SERVING: CALORIES: 303; FAT:3G; PROTEIN:0.5G; SUGAR:4G

Air Fryer Cinnamon Rolls

PREP: 15 MINUTES • COOK TIME: 5 MINUTES • TOTAL: 15 MINUTES
SERVES: 8

Ingredients
1 ½ tbsp. cinnamon
¾ C. brown sugar
¼ C. melted coconut oil
1 pound frozen bread dough, thawed

Glaze:
½ tsp. vanilla
1 ¼ C. powdered erythritol
2 tbsp. softened ghee
3 ounces softened cream cheese

Directions:
1. **Preparing the Ingredients.** Lay out bread dough and roll out into a rectangle. Brush melted ghee over dough and leave a 1-inch border along edges.
   Mix cinnamon and sweetener together and then sprinkle over the dough.
   Roll dough tightly and slice into 8 pieces. Let sit 1-2 hours to rise.
   To make the glaze, simply mix ingredients together till smooth.
2. **Air Frying.** Once rolls rise, place into the Air fryer oven and cook 5 minutes at 350 degrees.
   Serve rolls drizzled in cream cheese glaze. Enjoy!

PER SERVING: CALORIES: 390; FAT:8G; PROTEIN:1G; SUGAR:7G

Black and White Brownies

PREP: 10 MINUTES • COOK TIME: 20 MINUTES • TOTAL: 30 MINUTES
SERVES: 8

Ingredients
1 egg
¼ cup brown sugar
2 tablespoons white sugar
2 tablespoons safflower oil
1 teaspoon vanilla
¼ cup cocoa powder
⅓ cup all-purpose flour
¼ cup white chocolate chips
Nonstick baking spray with flour

Directions:
1. **Preparing the Ingredients.** In a medium bowl, beat the egg with the brown sugar and white sugar. Beat in the oil and vanilla.
   Add the cocoa powder and flour, and stir just until combined. Fold in the white chocolate chips.
   Spray a 6-by-6-by-2-inch baking pan with nonstick spray. Spoon the brownie batter into the pan.
2. **Air Frying.** Bake for 20 minutes or until the brownies are set when lightly touched with a finger. Let cool for 30 minutes before slicing to serve.

PER SERVING: CALORIES: 81; FAT:4G; PROTEIN:1G; FIBER:1G

Baked Apple

PREP: 5 MINUTES • COOK TIME: 20 MINUTES • TOTAL: 25 MINUTES
SERVES: 4

Ingredients
¼ C. water
¼ tsp. nutmeg
¼ tsp. cinnamon
1 ½ tsp. melted ghee
2 tbsp. raisins
2 tbsp. chopped walnuts
1 medium apple

Directions:
1. **Preparing the Ingredients.** Preheat your air fryer to 350 degrees.
   Slice an apple in half and discard some of the flesh from the center.
   Place into frying pan.
   Mix remaining ingredients together except water. Spoon mixture to the middle of apple halves.
   Pour water overfilled apples.
2. **Air Frying.** Place pan with apple halves into the Air fryer oven, bake 20 minutes.

PER SERVING: CALORIES: 199; FAT:9G; PROTEIN:1G; SUGAR:3G

Cinnamon Fried Bananas

PREP: 5 MINUTES • COOK TIME: 10 MINUTES • TOTAL: 15 MINUTES
SERVES: 2-3

Ingredients
1 C. panko breadcrumbs
3 tbsp. cinnamon
½ C. almond flour
3 egg whites
8 ripe bananas
3 tbsp. vegan coconut oil

Directions:
1. **Preparing the Ingredients**. Heat coconut oil and add breadcrumbs. Mix around 2-3 minutes until golden. Pour into bowl.
Peel and cut bananas in half. Roll each bananas half into flour, eggs, and crumb mixture.
2. **Air Frying.** Place into the Air fryer oven. Cook 10 minutes at 280 degrees.
A great addition to a healthy banana split!

PER SERVING: CALORIES: 219; FAT:10G; PROTEIN:3G; SUGAR:5G

HERITAGE OF FOOD: A FAMILY GATHERING

To survive, we need to eat. As a result, food has turned into a symbol of loving, nurturing and sharing with one another. Recording, collecting, sharing and remembering the recipes that have been passed to you by your family is a great way to immortalize and honor your family. It is these traditions that carve out your individual personality. You will not just be honoring your family tradition by cooking these recipes, but they will also inspire you to create your own variations, which you can then pass on to your children's.

The recipes are just passed on to everyone, and nobody actually possesses them. I too love sharing recipes. The collection is vibrant and rich as a number of home cooks have offered their inputs to ensure that all of us can cook delicious meals at our home. I am thankful to each one of you who has contributed to this book and has allowed their traditions to pass on and grow with others. You guys are wonderful!

I am also thankful to the cooks who have evaluated all these recipes. You're, as well as, the comments that came from your family members and friends were invaluable.

If you have the time and inclination, please consider leaving a short review wherever you can, we would love to learn more about your opinion.

https://www.amazon.com/review/review-your-purchases/

About the Author

Katherine is a New York-based food writer, experienced chef. She loves sharing Easy, Delicious and Healthy recipes, especially the delicious and healthy meals that can be prepared using her air fryer oven. Katherine is a passionate advocate for the health benefits of a low-carb lifestyle. When she's not cooking Katherine enjoys spending time with her husband and her kids, gardening and traveling.

Made in the USA
Middletown, DE
22 November 2019